CAUSES OF THE CONFLICT

Y OU COULD ARGUE THAT the American Revolution began in Philadelphia the day the Continental Congress adopted the Declaration of Independence. That was July 4, 1776. Or you could point to the first shot fired on Lexington Green during the early morning hours of April 19, 1775. Perhaps the Boston Massacre or the Tea Party was the start of it all. But if you want to understand the Revolution and why it happened—the causes—you have to go further back in time.

People often forget that the first European settlement on Manhattan Island was founded in 1614 by the Dutch, who called it New Amsterdam. The French, too, were early arrivals in the New World, establishing Port Royal, the first Canadian fur trading post, in 1605. The first permanent British settlement was made two years later at Jamestown in the colony of Virginia, named after the Virgin Queen, Elizabeth I.

George III became King of England in 1760. He had just turned twenty-two.

Peaceful coexistence, however, was not part of the British plan. Empire was on their minds, and in 1664, they eliminated the Dutch, capturing New Amsterdam and renaming it New York. Then, twenty-five years later, King William's War (1689-1697) marked the beginning of hostilities with the French. Usually, the fighting was part of a larger campaign being waged in Europe. Queen Anne's War (1702-1713), for instance, was the colonial component of the far larger War of the Spanish Succession, and King George's War (1744-1748) coincided with the War of the Austrian Succession. During each, professional British soldiers fought alongside the local colonial militias.

Paul Revere's engraving of "The Bloody Massacre" was a particularly effective piece of propaganda. Notice that the British officer, Captain Thomas Preston, is shown here ordering his redcoats to fire into the peaceful crowd. In fact, Preston was rescuing a sentry from an angry mob, and no account of the incident supports Revere's version.

Beginning in 1754, the French and Indian War (the Seven Years War in Europe) finally settled the issue. Its decisive North American battle was fought September 13, 1759, on the Plains of Abraham outside Quebec. There, French troops under the Marquis de Montcalm were defeated by a British expeditionary force under James Wolfe. Four years later, with the Treaty of Paris, France formally surrendered its remaining Canadian lands to the British. In the colonies, Americans celebrated in the streets, basking in the glory of an empire apparently at the height of its power.

Farmers and tanners, scribes and silversmiths. Pilgrims fleeing religious persecution and scoundrels fleeing the law. These were the men and women who braved a pitiless ocean to settle the New World. Some had come from England, and others had not. But the land they were living in was now unmistakably part of the British Empire. And so were they. Never was their allegiance to the Crown more strongly felt nor cherished so deeply as during the third year of the reign of His Majesty King George III. By a more conventional calendar, the date was 1763.

"When trade is at stake," William Pitt once said, "you must defend it or perish."

Unfortunately, as the euphoria of victory faded, it became clear that certain nagging problems remained unresolved.

Chief among them was the war debt. England's great victory had been engineered by Prime Minister William Pitt, who had steadfastly urged Parliament to outspend the French. Despite the warnings of his bookkeepers, Pitt had simply purchased, with whatever funds were available, enough men and matériel to ensure a British victory. When the books of account were totaled, however, the price for Pitt's victory came to £130 million.

This public debt was of great concern to George Grenville, the conservative financier who succeeded Pitt as prime minister. Grenville had an unshakable faith in the virtues of a balanced budget. It was said that he considered "a national saving of two inches of candle as a greater triumph than all Pitt's victories."

In an effort to raise some money, Parliament, at Grenville's suggestion, passed the Revenue Act of 1764, which came to be known as the Sugar Act. The name is a little misleading, however, because the Sugar Act called for new tariffs on a wide range of goods including sugar, textiles, indigo for dyeing, coffee, wine, and molasses. The preamble to the act makes its purpose explicitly clear: "It is just and necessary that a revenue be raised...in America for defraying the expenses of defending, protecting, and securing the same."

The Old State House dominates this view of Boston's State Street, which shows the active New England port as it looked during the second half of the eighteenth century.

Though Britain surely profited from her colonial trade, the colonies themselves were not cost-free possessions. Administering them, and maintaining a ten-thousand-man army there, were noticeable drains on an already depleted British treasury. Grenville was determined that the Americans should pay what he deemed to be their fair share.

In Grenville's defense, a tariff on molasses was nothing new. The Molasses Act of 1733, a law still on the books, imposed a duty of six pence per gallon on molasses. Which is not to say that colonial merchants actually paid this tariff. Usually, it was ignored. Sometimes officials were bribed.

The Sugar Act actually lowered the duty on molasses to three pence per gallon. But the new law had a hard edge to it, because this time Parliament meant to collect. Customs officials were sent packing to America with unambiguous orders: Get the money.

In the colonies, most of the opposition to the Sugar Act came from merchants who claimed that the new tariffs would hurt trade. Their arguments were strictly economic. Others, however, objected to the act on legal and philosophic grounds. The leaders of this group were an unlikely assortment of intellectuals and rabblerousers, who shared little more than an evolving American identity and a passion for self-rule.

The most outspoken and radical of these men was Samuel Adams of Boston. On May 24, 1764, Adams addressed a town meeting in Faneuil Hall on the subject of the Sugar Act. The new tariffs were improper, Adams argued, because they were being used not for trade regulation but to raise revenue. And if the British could tax molasses, he continued, what would stop them from taxing everything, including the farmers' own crops?

The crowd was not particularly receptive to Adams's denunciations of British policy, but his zealous associate, James Otis, did turn a phrase that would not soon be forgotten. In his speech entitled *Rights of the British Colonies Asserted and Proved*, Otis insisted that "no parts of His Majesty's dominions can be taxed without consent" and that "every part has a right to be represented in the supreme or some subordinate legislature...." Otis's argument was quickly distilled into a slogan that whipped through the thirteen colonies. The point was a simple one: No taxation without representation.

Printing this satire in its final issue, the Pennsylvania Journal *closed rather than purchase the hated stamps.*

Grenville thought Otis's argument to be absurd. Of course Britain had the right to tax its colonies in whatever manner it wished. But believing himself to be an astute judge of public sentiment, the prime minister proposed a substitute tax. After all, the money still had to be raised somehow.

In place of the Sugar Act, Grenville proposed the Stamp Act of 1765, which levied a tax on all paper goods and documents used in the colonies. School and college diplomas, for example, were taxed at two pounds each. Newspapers could only be printed on stamped paper taxed at one shilling per sheet, roughly what an army corporal made for a day's work. Even playing cards were taxed at one shilling per pack. In this way, Prime Minister Grenville hoped to spread the tax burden evenly throughout American colonial society. And furthermore, he indicated that the money the tax raised would be used exclusively for the protection of the colonies. What, Grenville thought, could be more fair?

A tax stamp. During the Stamp Act debate in Parliament, William Pitt found it necessary to remind his colleagues that "Americans are the sons, not the bastards of England."

America exploded. Stamp Act riots erupted in every port city up and down the eastern seaboard and inland as well. Opposition to the new law was spontaneous, violent, and universal. Every class and all political affiliations objected. Some called the new taxes robbery; others equated them to economic slavery. The only argument among the colonists was what to do about them.

Even Boston's Sons of Liberty, America's most overtly patriotic group, were stunned by the ferocity of the Stamp Act riots. On the night of August 14, 1765, a new brick building suspected of housing the stamp office was leveled, its wooden beams used to build a defiant bonfire. From the stamp office, the mob continued on to the house of Stamp Master Andrew Oliver. Oliver's house was spared demolition, but it was ransacked. And less than two weeks later, the house of Massachusetts Lieutenant Governor Thomas Hutchinson received similar treatment.

Obviously, something had to be done. Shaken by the violence, the royal governor, Francis Bernard, called out the colonial militia. But the colonel in charge had no intention of marching against the citizenry. In fact, he issued orders that any drummer attempting to sound the alarm should have his drum smashed. Boston was no longer under Bernard's control.

The Sons of Liberty refused any responsibility for the Stamp Act riots. For one thing, riots had occurred not only in Boston but throughout the colonies. And for another, the patriot leaders had never advocated violence. Even that notorious firebrand Sam Adams had championed a nonviolent response to the Stamp Act. Adams and his more reserved cousin John had written pamphlets decrying the tax and calling for all thirteen colonies to send delegates to a special conference in New York.

The Stamp Act Congress was a landmark gathering in the history of the American Revolution. Never before had the colonies joined together so effectively to express themselves with a common voice. A call in 1764 for such a congress to oppose the Sugar Act had fallen on unresponsive ears. But the Stamp Act was another matter entirely, and in October of 1765, twenty-seven delegates from nine colonies journeyed to New York to seek relief from Parliament. The delegates included both wealthy conservatives and fervent radicals. But they were all united in their opposition to the new taxes. They believed, as James Otis had argued, that the power to tax *in order to raise revenue* belonged properly to the colonists themselves and their own colonial legislatures.

It was this last argument that Grenville simply refused to understand: Under no circumstances would the colonists

This is an enlistment certificate of the type issued to British soldiers being sent to Boston. The date is 1765, the fifth year of his Majesty's reign, which was marked by the passage of the Stamp Act.

recognize Britain's right to tax them *in order to raise revenue*. Regulating trade was one thing, but revenue taxes such as the Stamp Act would not be tolerated. In fact, the colonists would not even allow the stamps to be distributed, turning back ships thought to be carrying them and raiding warehouses where they might be stored.

The Stamp Act Congress eventually issued thirteen "resolves." Among them, Resolves V and VI claimed for the colonial assemblies the exclusive right of taxation, and Resolves XI and XII urged the repeal of both the Stamp and Sugar Acts. But the resolves had much less practical effect than the mob violence. Once the royal governors informed Parliament that enforcement of the Stamp Act was impossible without a firm military commitment, the act was repealed. Had Parliament chosen instead to enforce the Stamp Act, the military phase of the American Revolution would have begun in 1766 and not nine years later.

News of the Stamp Act's repeal elated the Americans, who proclaimed loudly and often both their gratitude and their unceasing loyalty to the Crown. New York City even went so far as to erect a statue of George III on Bowling Green. Parliamentary hardliners, however, had exacted a small price for the repeal of the Stamp Act. This was the vaguely threatening Declaratory Act, which affirmed Parliament's right to make laws for the colonies "in all cases whatsoever." As it didn't cost the colonists anything, most saw little reason to complain.

For a time, the contentment of 1763 returned, at least on the surface. Americans chose to interpret the repeal of the Stamp Act as a Parliamentary admission that only colonial legislatures could raise revenue. But Parliament meant no such thing and quite the contrary. The repeal of the Stamp Act had been little more than an expedient retreat, and plans for new taxes were already under consideration. But the members of Parliament realized they would have to be more careful. The colonists had seen that united political action could force concessions. And this meant, the royal governors advised, that Britain could expect more fractious behavior from its colonists in the future.

General Thomas Gage (right) had been commander of the British forces in North America since 1763. Personally, he blamed the Stamp Act riots on the colonies' lawyers. "Without the Influence and Investigation of these inferior People," Gage wrote, the merchants "would have been quiet." It was the aftermath of the Townshend Acts, however, that forced Gage to send troops to Boston. The engraving by Revere (below) shows these redcoats landing at Long Wharf.

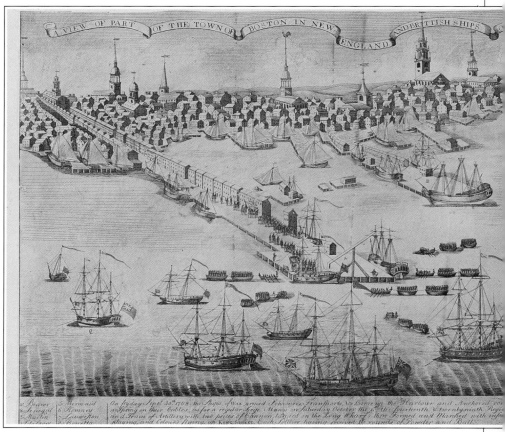

Of course, there was still the problem of paying for the British troops stationed in America. Early in 1766, soon after the repeal of the Stamp Act, the general in charge of these troops, Thomas Gage, began demanding funds for their support directly from the colonial legislatures. The Quartering Act, passed in 1765, had made the colonial authorities responsible for sheltering and supplying any troops quartered within their communities.

With some misgivings, the New York, New Jersey, and Pennsylvania legislatures acceded to Gage's demands. But when the call for funds was repeated the following year, New York reconsidered and refused the general's request. Because the greatest number of Gage's troops were quartered in New York, the legislature argued that it was being asked to bear an unfair share of the cost.

In Britain, there was pressure to charge those leading the resistance with high treason and ship them to England for trial. But cooler heads prevailed, and instead the New York legislature was suspended until it agreed to comply with the terms of the Quartering Act. Almost immediately, patriots in Boston announced a boycott of British goods in support of their sister colony. This, of course, did not help Britain's revenue situation.

In January of 1767, less than a year after the repeal of the Stamp Act, Chancellor of the Exchequer Charles Townshend announced to Parliament his intention to tax the colonies. In May, he proposed specifics. Townshend was careful to ignore the issue of whether Parliament had the right to enact a tax designed to raise revenue. Instead, he focused on the distinction made by some colonists, including Benjamin Franklin, between *internal* taxes and *external* tariffs. Townshend's plan was in many ways the Sugar Act revisited.

But the Townshend Acts were much more elaborate than a few simple tariffs. To begin with, they reduced North American troop strength by half, while shifting the cost of those soldiers who remained entirely onto the colonists. The Townshend Acts also provided for royal officials in the colonies to be paid directly by the Crown so that they would no longer be dependent on unfriendly legislatures for their salaries.

To finance these measures, Parliament imposed a new set of import duties on a few selected items—including paper, glass, and tea—that were much in demand. And to extend the enforcement powers of customs officials, "writs of assistance," or general search warrants, were made legal.

The colonial reaction was predictable, but less violent than it had been in response to the Stamp Act. This was due in part to the wisdom of experience, and in part to the fact that the Townshend Duties were, at first, very irregularly enforced. But on June 10, 1768, the British warship HMS *Romney* seized John Hancock's sloop *Liberty* on a charge of tax evasion.

Among the sources of young Hancock's wealth were shipping, smuggling, and a substantial inheritance from his uncle.

More than the tax charge was involved, however, as the circumstances of the seizure made clear. Obviously, the British were out to make a point. Hancock was one of the most popular and wealthy men in Boston—and quite likely a smuggler, too. But more importantly, he was a close ally of Sam Adams and the source of much Sons of Liberty funding.

The unruly mobs roaming the waterfront that night reminded Boston of what the Stamp Act riots had been like. Fearing for their lives, the customs commissioners fled to safety aboard the *Romney* and sent a message to Gage in New York advising him of the disorder "even to open revolt." Within a few days, however, the patriot leaders regained control and redirected the public outrage into more productive pursuits, such as another boycott of British goods intended to force repeal of the Townshend Duties.

In the matter of the *Liberty*, months of legal maneuvering followed. The case against Hancock would eventually be abandoned for lack of evidence, but in the meantime, Governor Bernard sent secret reports to Parliament calling for a dispatch of troops to Boston. Only a show of force, Bernard thought, could teach the colonists obedience. Bernard's request was unnecessary, however, because the decision had already been made. On September 29, 1768, three regiments of redcoats sailed into Boston Harbor.

The troops' presence was immediately and continuously disruptive. A thousand troops were not enough to cow sixteen thousand Bostonians, but they were more than enough to make trouble. Taunts were regularly exchanged, and to make matters worse, the poorly paid and generally off-duty British "lobsterbacks" competed with the townspeople for many of the same laborer's jobs. Pressure began to build.

In late February, 1770, an angry crowd surrounded the house of a customs informer named Ebenezer Richardson. When Richardson appeared at a window waving a musket, the mob threw stones and clods of dirt at him and knocked down his front door. Infuriated, Richardson fired. The first shot mortally wounded an eleven-year-old boy named Christopher Snider. The next day, two thousand Bostonians met under the Liberty Tree for the boy's funeral. Richardson's crime had little to do with the issue of British tyranny, but that was not what Sam Adams told the crowd. As far as this great manipulator of the popular will was concerned, of course the British were responsible.

In front of the Old State House, on the site of the Boston Massacre, is a plaque memorializing the event.

A little over a week later, the night of March 5, 1770, was cold and clear. An earlier snowfall had melted in spots during the day, freezing into ice by nightfall. Outside the Custom House, Private Hugh White took his turn at guard duty. Several wigmaker's apprentices spotted the lone sentry and began jeering him. White butted a particularly insulting boy with his gun, then chased and struck him again. As news of the attack spread—often exaggerated in the retelling—a crowd gathered around White. The new arrivals were men, not boys, and there were perhaps two hundred of them in a very hostile mood. "Fire!" some of them screamed. "Just fire!" Frightened and confused, Private White called to a nearby barracks for help.

The captain of the day, Thomas Preston, was an experienced officer who knew what might happen if he called out the entire regiment. But the Custom House was an important repository of confidential records, and there was also White's personal safety to be considered. In the end, Preston chose a middle course, personally leading a squad of seven men to rescue White.

The scene in front of the Custom House was one of chaos. People pushed and shouted as bells rang and dogs barked. Preston and his squad made it to the sentry post without incident. But when they tried to withdraw, bodies closed in around them. The soldiers tried to force their way out, but the crowd was unyielding. Next, Preston ordered his men to form a defensive arc while he tried to persuade the people to disperse.

This stone marks the tomb of the five men killed in the Boston Massacre. Among them, Crispus Attucks was a black man who had emigrated from the Bahamas. More than twelve thousand people, three-quarters of the city's population, turned out for the funeral.

Preston's task was hopeless. The yelling grew louder as close to four hundred menacing patriots pressed close against the redcoats' extended bayonets. The soldiers loaded their muskets. Then a club was thrown by someone in the crowd. It knocked down a soldier. His gun went off—perhaps intentionally, perhaps not. The shot hit no one. But another shot was fired, and Sam Gray fell to the ice with a gaping hole in his head. More shots, all fired without orders from Preston, killed four more civilians and wounded six. It was a "massacre," Sam Adams said.

Ironically, March 5, 1770, was also the date that Parliament repealed the Townshend Duties. An American boycott of British goods, arranged through a series of colonial "nonimportation" agreements, had defeated the revenue-raising goals of the tariffs. In their first year, for example, the Townshend Duties had raised £295, while sending troops to Boston as an enforcement tool had cost the treasury £170,000. The economics of the situation made the law's repeal inevitable. But for the sake of British pride, King George personally insisted that one duty remain: the tariff on tea.

Despite the Massacre, the repeal of the Townshend Duties quieted Boston for a time. The tariff on tea could be avoided easily enough by drinking smuggled Dutch tea, and a relative calm prevailed until 1773, when Parliament decided to grant the ailing East India Company a monopoly on the colonial tea trade.

As usual, Britain's unfortunate tendency to act arbitrarily in colonial matters could be counted on to gall the Sons of Liberty. This time, the Boston patriots announced that as long as the monopoly remained in effect, no East India

On the Death of Five young Men who was Murthered, March 5th 1770. By the 29th Regiment.

Before the chests of East India Company tea were thrown overboard, they were first cut and split with tomahawks.

Company ship would be permitted to land in Boston. When the first ships arrived in early December, the threat was repeated. Then, on the night of December 16, 1773, it was carried out. A band of Bostonians dressed as Mohawk Indians, their cheeks darkened with burnt cork, boarded the tea ships and dumped their cargo. The 340 chests of East India Company tea were worth about £9,000 on the open market.

Following Massachusetts' lead, patriots in New York burnt a consignment of East India Company tea, while in Maryland, an entire ship was destroyed along with its cargo. In South Carolina, East India Company tea was confiscated and sold to pay for other rebellious activities. Parliament was aghast. There was no way these open acts of rebellion could go unpunished.

Parliament's response was a collection of new laws, known as the Coercive Acts in London and the Intolerable Acts here. Among their provisions, the Coercive Acts compelled Boston to make restitution for the ruined tea. The Boston Port Bill specifically closed Boston Harbor, choking trade and the local economy, while the Massachusetts Government Act ended for all practical purposes colonial self-rule. In the meantime, General Gage had been appointed royal governor of Massachusetts so that he could personally enforce the Port Bill. Though many had condemned the Tea Party as an act of vandalism, the Coercive Acts forced Bostonians to choose sides. A few wealthy conservatives, known as Tories, remained loyal to the Crown, but most townspeople rallied around the Sons of Liberty.

Patriots in other colonies also pledged their support to the Massachusetts radicals. Donations of food, livestock, and money were sent—anything that could be spared. And with this support, Boston refused to back down. The patriots' resolve forced Gage, irrevocably committed to a show of British strength, to request more troops. New regiments arrived in June, 1774, bringing to four thousand the total number of redcoats in the city, or one soldier for every four civilians.

To protect themselves, the Massachusetts colonists began to purge Tory sympathizers from the officer corps of the local militias. They also formed one-quarter of their militias into special companies that would drill two or three times a week. Because these companies were designed to be ready at a moment's notice, they were known as "Minute Men."

Hoping to forestall an armed conflict, conservatives in New York called for another colonial conference along the lines of the Stamp Act Congress. Their goal was to convince Boston to repay the East India Company for its lost tea. But by the time the First Continental Congress met on September 5, 1774, at Carpenter's Hall in Philadelphia, appeasement was no longer a workable course of action. Though most of the delegates still paid lip service to the Crown, Patrick Henry proclaimed, "The distinctions between Virginians, Pennsylvanians, New Yorkers, and New Englanders are no more. I am not a Virginian, but an American."

After seven weeks of often heated debate, the delegates approved a series of strong resolves. They specifically demanded the repeal of the Coercive Acts and the recall of British troops posted in Boston. To force these issues, the Congress also called for continued and more extensive boycotts of British goods and agreed to meet again a year later if Parliament had not complied with its demands.

THE FIRST SHOT

DURING THE CIVIL RIGHTS MOVEMENT of the 1960s, whites in southern towns would often blame "northern agitators" for the growth of black political activism. They simply couldn't accept the reality that southern blacks themselves understood and wanted change. In much the same way, the British of 1775 refused to accept that the mass of colonists had turned against them. If only a few bad apples, such as Sam Adams and John Hancock, could be removed, the British believed, the rest of the crop could be saved.

Following this view, Lord Dartmouth, the cabinet minister for colonial affairs, ordered the arrest of Adams and Hancock on January 27, 1775. He actually believed their capture would quash the rebellion.

That spring, Boston was overpopulated with spies, both British and American. Gage's army made the city a bit too hot for the patriot leaders, who removed themselves to the countryside. But enough Sons of Liberty remained in town to keep watch over the British and report their troop movements. At the same time, Tories infiltrated patriot councils in order to discover the rebels' plans.

During this time, Gage was under considerable pressure. Suffering under the colonies' nonimportation agreements, London's merchants pressed Parliament for a solution to the stalemate. And Parliament, having provided Gage with an expensive army of more than four thousand troops, pressed the general for results. But on the ground in Boston, Gage knew that one misstep could trigger a shooting war.

Rather than chase Adams and Hancock, Gage pursued what he believed to be a less inflammatory course of action. His intelligence officers had learned of a large store of colo-

nial munitions eighteen miles away at Concord. During the second week of April, 1775, Gage decided to seize it. First, he relieved the most elite British companies, the light infantry and the grenadiers, of their garrison duties. Then he secretly reformed them into a striking force of 750 men under Lieutenant Colonel Francis Smith. On the night of April 18, all was ready. Under the cover of darkness, the redcoats crossed the Charles River by longboat and marched on Concord.

Gage had counted on the element of surprise, but of course there would be none. American spies, among them Paul Revere, had noticed immediately the change in grenadier and light infantry routine. In fact, on April 15, the leader of the patriots still in Boston, Dr. Joseph Warren, had sent Revere to Lexington to warn Adams and Hancock. On his return, Revere paused in Charlestown. There, according to his own report, Revere "agreed with a Colonel Conant and some other gentlemen that if the British went out by water, we [in Boston] would show two lanterns in the North Church Steeple; and if by land, one as a signal; for we were apprehensive it would be difficult [for a messenger] to cross the Charles River or get over Boston Neck."

On Tuesday night, the 18th, around ten o'clock, Warren again called for Revere. Soldiers had been seen marching down to the common, and Warren had already sent William Dawes to warn Lexington and Concord by an overland route across Boston Neck. Revere was sent in great haste by the quicker "sea" route, which the British themselves had taken. Pausing long enough to arrange for two lanterns to be hung in the North Church steeple—briefly, so as not to attract attention—Revere set out with two oarsmen for the Charlestown side.

Somehow slipping past the HMS *Somerset* moored in the mouth of the Charles River, Revere was met on the Charlestown shore by several patriots who had seen the

In order to hang the lanterns that signaled British movement by sea, one of Revere's spies had to sneak quietly out of a boarding house filled with redcoats.

This statue by Daniel Chester French, entitled "Minute Man," today guards the North Bridge in Concord. There, wrote Ralph Waldo Emerson, "By the rude bridge that arched the flood / Their flag to April's breeze unfurled/ Here the embattled farmers stood/ And fired the shot heard 'round the world."

With Adams and Hancock out of town, Dr. Joseph Warren became the patriots' chief of staff in Boston, making his informal headquarters at the Green Dragon Tavern.

North Church signal. The time was nearly eleven o'clock. Given a fast horse, Revere set off immediately for Lexington. Crossing Charlestown Neck, he was nearly captured by two patrolling British officers. But able to outrun them, Revere soon reached Medford, where he awakened the captain of the Minute Men. Continuing along, he alarmed nearly every house he passed on his way.

It was close to midnight when Revere breathlessly reined in his horse beside the house of the Reverend Jonas Clarke, where Adams and Hancock were lodging. At first, one of the men guarding the house, Sergeant William Munroe, told Revere to keep down the noise lest it waken those sleeping inside. "Noise!" Revere boomed. "You'll have noise enough before long. The regulars are coming out!"

The British meanwhile had landed in a marsh, which slowed their advance considerably. Then, upon reaching dry land, they tarried awhile in a pointless attempt to dry themselves. Not until dawn did the advance troops under Major John Pitcairn reach Lexington Green. There, waiting for them, were about seventy Minute Men under Captain John Parker. Quaking from fear if not the cold, Parker's two companies were more defiant than threatening. Fathers and sons stood side by side in homespun breeches, while some of the older men carried muskets they had used in the French and Indian War.

Because Parker's men were actually off to the side of the road, Pitcairn's column could have marched straight through town without challenging them. Instead, the major confronted the Minute Men and ordered them to disperse. A first shot rang out. Each side later accused the other of firing it. In any case, it resulted in a fusillade from the British.

The redcoat soldiers were under orders not to fire, but they were tired, frightened, and poorly led. Having been drawn from different regiments, the companies of grenadiers and light infantry had never trained together. Himself an officer in the Royal Marines, Pitcairn aggravated the situation by issuing conflicting orders. He told the Minute Men to disperse, but his own men he ordered to surround and capture the Lexington militia. And once the first shot was fired, shooting back seemed both a logical and natural reaction.

The fighting was over within minutes, as the outgunned Minute Men hastily withdrew. But in that time, eight Americans were killed on the green. Only one British soldier was wounded.

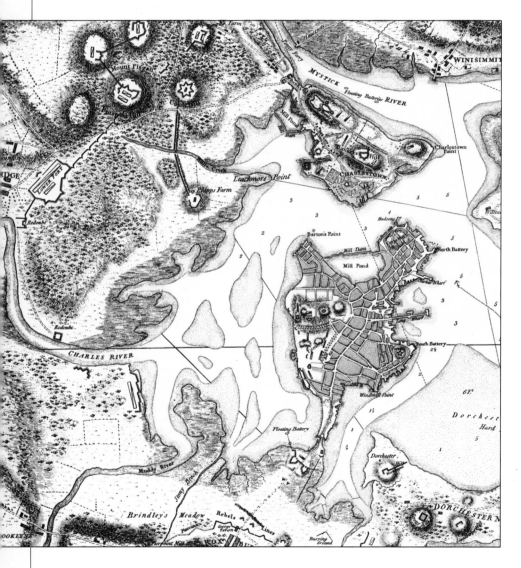

Boston and its environs. Although the geography of Boston made it an excellent port for oceangoing commerce, the city itself was hardly the most defensible spot for the British to have quartered such a large army. The slender napes of Boston Neck to the south and Charlestown Neck across the river threatened to bottle up any soldiers that might be concentrated on the two peninsulas. The high ground around Boston also provided many opportunities for the advantageous placement of besieging artillery. Breed's and Bunker Hill above Charlestown (transposed on this map, as on many others) and the Dorchester Heights below Boston offered particularly commanding positions.

Adams and Hancock heard the shots from their coach as they rode out of town. Realizing the significance of this first volley, Adams proclaimed, "What a glorious morning for America!"

Pitcairn and Smith continued on to Concord, where they began a house-by-house search for arms and ammunition. Having received intelligence that additional stores were hidden at Colonel James Barrett's farm north of the town, Smith sent a detachment of troops across the North Bridge to destroy anything they could find. Three companies were left behind to guard the bridge.

In the meantime, having heard of the events in Lexington, militiamen from the surrounding countryside began gathering on Punkatasset Hill outside Concord. A general mood of indecision prevailed until smoke was seen rising from the town. Although the source was a bonfire of weaponry, the Concord militiamen feared their homes were being put to the torch. Heading back toward town, they and their fellows advanced on the British companies at North Bridge. At first, the British withdrew; then, as the Americans continued to advance, the British fired. When the Americans returned the fire, three redcoats were killed, the first British fatalities of the war. Outnumbered four to one, the bridge guard retreated to the center of town.

During the next two hours, Smith regrouped his command and attended to the dead and wounded. Then he set off for Boston. All the way back to Lexington, Smith's troops were harassed by hundreds of militiamen hiding behind buildings, stone walls, fences, and trees. Flanking parties generally kept the snipers at a comfortable distance. But when the road narrowed, forcing in the British flanks, the Americans did enjoy some measure of success.

About 2:30 P.M., Smith reached Lexington, where he was joined by a thousand reinforcements under the command of Hugh, Lord Percy. Taking the opportunity afforded him by the might of Percy's column, Smith rested his men briefly before beginning the final leg of the retreat.

Even with these reinforcements, the Americans still outnumbered the British by about two to one. But Percy's troops had brought cannon with them, which were used to disperse the massing Americans.

Without these cannon, Smith and Percy might not have made it back to Boston. As it was, they crossed Charlestown Neck after nightfall, camping near Bunker Hill where the guns of the *Somerset* could protect them. Total British casualties were 73 dead, 174 wounded, 26

The first fight at the North Bridge in Concord took place on April 19, 1775. Since then, there have been many reenactments. This one was photographed at the turn of the century for a set of picture postcards.

missing. The Americans lost 49 men, with 40 wounded and 5 missing.

But the casualty figures don't tell the full story. The fighting also had the effect of transforming Gage from the royal governor of a colony into the commanding general of an occupied town. Inspired by the bravery of the local companies, militia units from all over New England, and as far away as Pennsylvania and New York, rallied at Cambridge. Not strong enough to take on Gage's men, they nevertheless deterred further British expeditions into the countryside and, in fact, besieged the city.

The men who flocked to Cambridge were exceptionally high in morale, but nearly as low in supplies. Dressed in plain clothes, they had little ammunition, almost no artillery, and not much food to eat. To relieve their situation, an ambitious Connecticut patriot named Benedict Arnold devised a bold plan.

Arnold proposed to the governing Massachusetts Committee of Safety that he lead a force to capture Fort Ticonderoga at the southern tip of Lake Champlain. The fort was the strategic focus of the traditional Champlain-Hudson invasion route from Canada, and among its great treasures was a store of heavy cannon. Best of all, Arnold claimed, Ticonderoga was an easy target. Because the French no longer occupied Canada, the fort had become principally a frontier police station, with a light garrison of just under fifty men.

The Committee of Safety initially backed the idea, making Arnold a provisional colonel, but it hesitated when someone pointed out that the fort lay within the colony of New York and thus outside Massachusetts' jurisdiction. The headstrong Arnold, however, had no intention of waiting while the Committee discussed the matter with its neighbor. Instead, he set off on a reconnaissance mission,

instructing the Committee to muster an army and send it after him.

In the meantime, another force was marching on Ticonderoga. Led by Ethan Allen of the Hampshire Grants (now Vermont), these men were known as the Green Mountain Boys. Arnold caught up with Allen at a small country tavern. Though still without a command of his own, Arnold presented Allen with his commission from the Committee of Safety and insisted on taking charge of the expedition. Allen thought Arnold must be either joking or crazy. The Green Mountain Boys, three hundred strong, would certainly not march under anyone else's orders, especially not those of this arrogant unknown. But Arnold, continually citing his credentials, pressed his argument, and soon the pair disappeared into a back room. When they emerged, the expedition had two leaders.

T he capture of the fort was even simpler than anticipated. Early on the morning of May 10, 1775, Allen's men landed on the western shore of Lake Champlain, about a thousand yards above the fort. Arnold tried one last time to assume sole command. But Allen replied that if Arnold didn't shut up, he'd be clapped in irons. That settled the matter, and they continued on to the fort. Its gates were guarded only by a dozing sentry.

Taking Ticonderoga without firing a shot, Allen raced up a flight of stairs to the commanding officer's quarters, shouting to him with a definite lack of military protocol, "Come out, you old rat!" Captain William De la Place refused to appear until he had time to dress, so it was left to Lieutenant Jocelyn Feltham, himself disrobed, to confront the Americans. According to Allen's account, Feltham demanded by what authority he surrender the fort. "In the name of the great Jehovah and the Continental Congress," Allen roared, or so he claimed. But Feltham remembered the scene differently. According to the British lieutenant, Arnold did most of the talking, and Allen said no such thing. Whatever really happened, it mattered little to Allen's legend. The capture of Ticonderoga was particularly notable in that it was the Americans' first offensive action,

This engraving shows Ethan Allen making his legendary speech invoking God and the body politic. According to the British, however, Arnold did the talking. Lt. Feltham reported: "Mr. Arnold told me...he must have immediate possession of the fort and all the effects of George the Third."

George Washington's first taste of battle came in May, 1754. Sent with some militia to secure the Ohio River, he met a party of adventuring Frenchmen and ordered his men to fire. It was the first engagement of the French and Indian War.

Lexington and Concord having been defensive fights. It was also the last time colonial military commanders would act without the official sanction of the Continental Congress, which had just reconvened. The political climate in Philadelphia having changed, the Second Continental Congress was able to move its deliberations from Carpenters' Hall to the well-appointed Pennsylvania State House, the building known today as Independence Hall.

In the aftermath of Lexington, Concord, and now Ticonderoga, the most pressing business before the Congress was the chartering of an American army and the selection of its commander. John Hancock clearly craved the position, but even his allies Sam and John Adams understood that Hancock, being so strongly identified with Massachusetts, would be an unpopular choice. Instead, seeking some measure of regional solidarity, John Adams nominated a Virginia farmer active in the patriot cause since the Stamp Act Congress. Taken on June 15, the vote for George Washington's appointment as commander-in-chief of the Continental Army was unanimous.

A modest man by nature, Washington accepted the position reluctantly. He had served as an officer with the British during the French and Indian War, but his far greater concern was the state of the troops, which comprised an army in name only.

Made up of the various militia and volunteer units encamped at Cambridge, the men had already fought one battle at Bunker Hill. The bad news was they lost the hill. The good news was the British had paid a shocking price.

In late May of 1775, Gage had been joined by three major generals—John Burgoyne, Henry Clinton, and William Howe—sent by Parliament to assist him in suppressing the rebellion. Howe promptly devised a plan to storm the American encampment at Cambridge. But word

One of the last men to retreat from Breed's Hill, Col. Prescott refused to run. From time to time, however, he was forced to stop walking, turn, and defend himself.

of Howe's plan leaked, of course, and the Committee of Safety decided to preempt the British by fortifying Bunker Hill on the Charlestown peninsula. There was no unified command, but those in leadership roles included Colonel William Prescott of the Massachusetts militia, General Israel Putnam of the Connecticut militia, and Richard Gridley, a retired colonel with considerable engineering experience.

Prescott led a force of twelve hundred men out of Cambridge at nine o'clock on the evening of June 16. Putnam met the column at Charlestown with several wagonloads of picks and shovels. Prescott, Putnam, and Gridley conferred. At first, they discussed which of the three hills they were supposed to fortify. Putnam and Gridley wanted to fortify the large hill closest to Boston. But Prescott was convinced that Bunker Hill was, in fact, the taller hill behind it, and his orders said *Bunker* Hill. Putnam and Gridley argued that whatever its name, the closer hill (actually Breed's Hill) was the one to fortify. They argued for an hour before Prescott relented.

First light revealed the Americans and drew harassing fire from British ships in the harbor. At a council of war that morning, Gage and the other generals agreed that the Americans had to be removed from the Charlestown peninsula. Clinton suggested a landing near Charlestown Neck. Threatening to cut off their only means of retreat, he reasoned, would certainly send the Americans scurrying back to the mainland. Clinton's plan was brushed aside, however, in favor of a direct assault on the hill recommended by Howe.

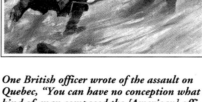

This wooden compass, part of the exhaustive Neumann Collection at Valley Forge, was manufactured in France around 1760.

Gage sided with Howe for two reasons. The first was his fear of placing British troops in between two American forces, one on the mainland and the other occupying the peninsula. Gage's second reason was his belief that Howe's plan would achieve an important propaganda goal: a no-nonsense thrashing of the uppity colonists.

The attack was to begin as soon as possible, but mustering and transporting the troops took the entire morning. By the time Howe and his fifteen hundred light infantry and grenadiers had crossed the harbor, it was already well past noon. On Breed's Hill, the Americans had used the intervening hours well, strengthening their earthworks considerably. The fortified wall, or redoubt, they had constructed was now quite sturdy, though its flanks were suspect. Fortunately for the Americans, Howe planned a straight-on frontal assault featuring those beautiful troop lines so admired by military leaders of the eighteenth century.

It was not a good plan. Moving through long grass and carrying sixty-pound packs that slowed their charge, the British soldiers were decimated by American volleys. In order to conserve their precious supply of musket balls and powder, the Americans were ordered by Putnam not to fire at the British until they could see the "whites of their eyes." The neat lines of redcoats fell in grisly, bloody heaps.

Bravely, Howe gathered up his retreating forces at the bottom of the hill and reformed their lines. Then he sent them up the hill again. Once more, American fire ripped the British to pieces. But this second assault all but exhausted the Americans' ammunition. There was enough left to damage, but not repel, a third wave. Yet the Americans held their ground. And the British came again.

It was only after the Americans had finally run out of ammunition that the British were able to breach the

redoubt. And then, only when the fighting turned hand-to-hand, did Prescott order a retreat.

Of the 2,200 British soldiers, including reinforcements, who fought that day, half were wounded, 226 of them fatally. The Americans lost about 140 men, with about double that number wounded. Major John Pitcairn, who had led the British at Lexington, and Dr. Joseph Warren, serving as a major general in the Massachusetts militia, were among the dead.

Meanwhile, consideration was being given to the military situation in the north. Inflamed by his success at Ticonderoga, Benedict Arnold proposed in late June an even more ambitious enterprise: the invasion of Canada. Arnold argued for an immediate attack, before reinforcements could arrive from England. The Continental Congress agreed. General Philip Schuyler would follow Lake Champlain north, attacking Montreal, while Arnold would take a daring route through the Maine wilderness to the Canadian border, where he would join Schuyler. Together, they would march on the British stronghold at Quebec.

On September 4, Schuyler set off northward down Champlain, but a week later illness forced him to surrender his command to Richard Montgomery and return to Ticonderoga. The younger and more vigorous Montgomery pressed forward and on September 16 began siege operations at St. Johns, a British fort on the Richelieu River that guarded access to the St. Lawrence River and Quebec beyond.

One British officer wrote of the assault on Quebec, "You can have no conception what kind of man composed the [American] officers. Of those we took, one major was a blacksmith, another a hatter."

The siege took much longer than expected. Not until November 2 did the garrison at St. John's surrender. In the meantime, frustrated by the delay, Ethan Allen recruited his own "army" of 110 rebellious Canadians and quixotically marched on Montreal, a city of 5,000. Another band of 200 Canadians under Major John Brown was to join him there, but Brown and his men never appeared. Additionally, Allen had counted on a popular uprising within the town, but Montreal's citizens remained loyal to the Crown. After a brief engagement, Allen was captured and shipped to England as a prisoner of war. Montgomery's force eventually took Montreal on November 22.

Further north and east, Arnold was discovering that the backwoods of Maine were much more brutal than he had anticipated. The first few weeks traveling up the Kennebec River had been slow but smooth, with abundant wild game and much local corn. But as winter came, conditions worsened drastically. Many of Arnold's boats were smashed during portages through the woods, and much food was lost. By late October, the men were eating soap. When that ran out, the soldiers turned to shoe leather, cartridge boxes, and the company dog. What had begun as one of the most ambitious marches in military history turned into one of the most punishing. Only the relief offered by friendly Canadians at the border saved Arnold's command from being completely wiped out.

With fewer than one thousand men, Arnold and Montgomery attacked Quebec between four and five in the morning on New Year's Day, 1776, during a raging blizzard. They were counting on a surprise, because the odds were heavily against them. Quebec was one of the best fortified cities in North America. And what made matters worse was the garrison of two thousand men who, unlike the Americans, were healthy, warm, and well fed. Still, the Americans fought cleverly and well. Arnold's plan called for a feint along the front lines, while both Arnold and Montgomery slipped along the city walls, converging on the waterfront at the rear of the city's Lower Town.

The plan might have worked had Montgomery not been killed and Arnold not wounded. The Americans actually captured a passageway that would have given them unimpeded access to the city. But in the absence of decisive leadership, rather than storm through the gates into Quebec's interior, the troops waited outside for orders that never came. In time, the British regrouped, and the opening became a trap. At 9:00 A.M., the last of the Americans surrendered.

Of course, Washington had problems of his own. When he had first arrived at Cambridge that summer, morale had been high. The stories of Lexington, Concord, and Bunker Hill had inspired thousands of everyday Americans to take up the cause of liberty. But as summer slipped into fall and winter, spirits waned. Washington poked at the British, and the British under "Gentleman Johnny" Burgoyne poked back. Other than this occasional skirmishing, there was little to do but loiter about camp. Despising the monotony as

much as the meager supplies, most of the enlisted men planned to quit as soon as their six-month hitches were up. Consequently, by February, 1776, Washington's army had shrunk to less than half the soldiers promised him by the Continental Congress.

Needless to say, calling them soldiers was somewhat charitable. Aroused by the language of independence, many were unruly libertarians with little respect for authority of any kind, British or otherwise. Once Washington faced up to the task of convincing them to reenlist, he then had to make soldiers out of them. Which chore was more difficult, even the general couldn't say. Both were intractable problems that would plague him throughout his years as commander-in-chief.

Washington's immediate task was to drive the British out of Boston, but for that he needed heavy cannon of the type captured at Ticonderoga and nearby Crown Point. As the winter stalemate stretched on, Washington sent bookseller and amateur artillery expert Henry Knox to fetch the Ticonderoga cannon and bring them to Boston. Attempting to drag bronze and cast-iron cannon through the Berkshire Mountains during the coldest part of the winter was nothing short of heroic, but somehow Knox managed it. And when the spring thaw came, the British awoke one morning to find their own cannon pointing at them from atop Dorchester Heights.

Howe, who had replaced Gage as commander-in-chief, saw that Boston was now lost to him, so he proposed a deal. If Washington would allow the British troops to board their ships unmolested, Howe would not burn Boston. With Washington's agreement, Sir William loaded nearly 9,000 soldiers onto 125 vessels and evacuated Boston on March 17, 1776. Howe made for Halifax, Nova Scotia. But Washington, thinking the general would head for New York, sent his own army south.

This British cartoon took on both the English military, ridiculing its "victory" at Bunker Hill, and contemporary coiffures.

INDEPENDENCE

The Liberty Bell was cast in 1752 to hang in Independence Hall (left). It cracked while being tested, was recast, and then cracked again.

F ROM THE BANKS OF the Thames River where Parliament sat, things did not appear to be going well in the northern colonies. Frankly, the events at Concord and Bunker Hill had shocked the British. Decrying these near defeats, London's newspapers mocked the government's handling of the crisis. In his office in Whitehall, Lord Dartmouth, secretary of state for the colonies, searched for something else to try.

The southern colonies seemed an inviting alternative to stubborn, puritan Massachusetts. There had been reports for some time that Loyalists in Georgia and the Carolinas were abundant and strongly supported the Crown. All they lacked, it was said, was some indication of British support.

The signal the British sent was unmistakable. On January 6, 1776, Henry Clinton was ordered to leave Boston and take command of a combined military and naval force for the purpose of besieging Charleston, South Carolina. Serving under Clinton were Admiral Peter Parker and Charles, Lord Cornwallis. Clinton's orders were to secure Georgia, the Carolinas, and Virginia—putting Loyalists in charge as necessary, and then rejoining Howe as soon as possible in the north.

In support of Clinton's action, though somewhat prematurely, Governor Josiah Martin of North Carolina raised a hefty force of some sixteen hundred men, which marched to the coast under the command of Donald McDonald. Plans called for a rendezvous with General Clinton near Cape Fear. But along the way, the column was intercepted on February 27, 1776, by eleven hundred patriot militia at Moore's Creek Bridge. In a brief but decisive battle, the Loyalist force was routed and McDonald captured.

Clinton learned this distressing news when his ship arrived at Cape Fear on March 12. Without the local support promised him, the general had little choice but to wait for Parker's delayed fleet, which finally arrived from Ireland at the end of May.

Expecting an attack, the people of Charleston used this time productively. Cannon emplacements were built, and fortifications erected. Under the leadership of Colonel William Moultrie, a fort was quickly constructed on Sullivan's Island at the entrance to Charleston Harbor. Though forts designed to withstand cannon fire were often built with heavy masonry walls, Moultrie was forced to make do with rubbery palmetto logs.

On June 4, 1776, General Charles Lee made his own much-delayed appearance to supervise Charleston's defense. Though the Continental Congress thought well enough of Lee's military ability to place him in command of the Southern Department, his colleagues knew him to be a crotchety, self-absorbed officer, lazy, and not much liked. He immediately chastised Moultrie for the construction of Fort Sullivan, which he called indefensible and "a slaughter-pen." Lee then proceeded to issue a barrage of orders, some foolish and others dangerous, which were mostly ignored by

The attack on Fort Sullivan. Wrote one of Moultrie's men, "The expression of a Sergeant McDaniel, after a cannon ball had taken off his shoulder..., is worth recording in the annals of America: 'Fight on, my brave boys! Don't let liberty expire with me today!'"

the Carolinians. When Moultrie refused to comply, Lee undertook to relieve him of his Sullivan's Island command. Just then, the British attacked.

On June 16, Clinton landed twenty-five hundred men on Long Island, a narrow slip divided from Sullivan's Island by a stretch of shallows called the Breach. Clinton was assured that his men could easily ford the Breach at low tide. But on reaching the island, he was startled to discover the Breach was pitted with potholes up to seven feet deep. This meant his troops were effectively marooned there.

Quite happy now that the glory would be his alone, a confident Parker made plans for a naval assault on Fort Sullivan. The attack was scheduled for June 23, but adverse winds forced him to wait five days. On the morning of June 28, Parker's frigates opened fire. With an over-whelming advantage in firepower, the admiral anticipated a convincing victory.

But what Parker, and even Moultrie, never expected was that the peculiar construction of Fort Sullivan made it nearly impervious to cannon fire. Set into a sand buffer, the elastic palmetto logs absorbed the shock of cannon fire that would have, in other circumstances, blown down heavier mortar walls. Moultrie wrote later that his casualties resulted almost exclusively from shots that passed through the fort's embrasures.

Parker was not so lucky. Though chronically short of ammunition, Moultrie directed his fire carefully, holding the fort and inflicting heavy losses on the British ships, especially Parker's flagship. One cannonball came so close to the admiral's person that it caught the tail of Parker's coat and ripped his breeches clean off his body. By evening, the British were forced to retire, abandoning their plans for a quick conquest of the south.

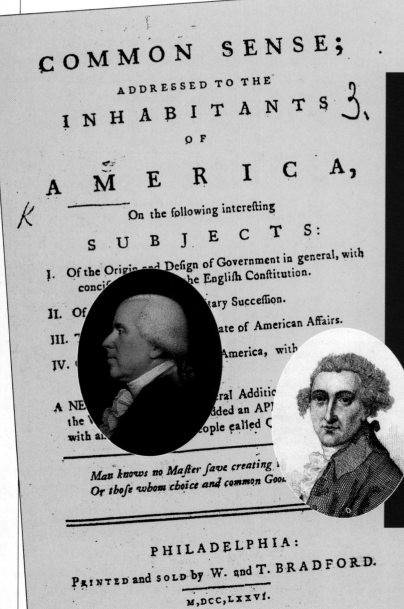

COMMON SENSE;

ADDRESSED TO THE

INHABITANTS

OF

AMERICA,

On the following interesting

SUBJECTS:

I. Of the Origin and Design of Government in general, with conci... the English Constitution.

II. Of ... tary Succession.

III. ...ate of American Affairs.

IV. ... America, with

A NE... ral Additio...
the ... dded an API...
with a... ople called C...

Man knows no Master save creating ...
Or those whom choice and common Goo...

PHILADELPHIA:

Printed and sold by W. and T. BRADFORD.

M,DCC,LXXVI.

[Price one British Shilling.]

LIKE MANY IN THE VANGUARD of the American Revolution, Thomas Paine came to politics after attempting a variety of trades. An Englishman by birth, he had been a corset-maker, a schoolteacher, a tobacconist, and a grocer. Paine had also been a tax collector until he was dismissed for leading his colleagues in a call for higher wages. Bankrupt and aimless, he attracted the attention of Benjamin Franklin, who encouraged him to start his life over again in America. Provided by Franklin with a letter of introduction, Paine left for Philadelphia in 1774.

There Paine met Dr. Benjamin Rush, a radical patriot, who asked him to write an essay justifying the need for independence. Rush had himself been working on such an essay, but he feared professional reprisals from the conservative elements in Philadelphia, where he had roots. If Paine's essay caused trouble, however, the rootless, revolutionary Englishman could simply move on to more congenial territory in Massachusetts.

The pamphlet Paine wrote—*Common Sense*—quickly became, with the possible exception of the Holy Bible, the most widely read piece of writing in the colonies. Published in Philadelphia on January 9, 1776, *Common Sense* was read by upwards of one million Americans, fully half the colonial population at the time.

An impassioned treatise on the rights of man, *Common Sense* may have included some shoddy philosophizing, but the booklet truly reached its public. Avoiding scholarly jargon, Paine expressed his ideas in a language that was filled with the passion and determination of his readership. "The sun never shined on a cause of greater worth," Paine wrote.

A self-educated man, Thomas Paine (right) failed at one job after another until Dr. Benjamin Rush (left), Philadelphia's most progressive physician, suggested that he try his hand at professional revolution, pamphlets his specialty.

Above: Thomas Jefferson (left) and Richard Henry Lee (center) of Virginia pose beside John Adams (right) of Massachusetts. Below: This painting by John Trumbull was the first to depict the signing of the Declaration of Independence. Because Trumbull worked a generation later, however, and was not present at the signing, his rendering of the scene may not be historically accurate.

A year after Lexington and Concord, the Americans knew what they were fighting against—British tyranny. But what were they fighting for?

Virginian Richard Henry Lee provided the answer. When the Continental Congress reconvened in May, 1776, Lee proposed that his fellow delegates declare "these United Colonies are, and of right ought to be, free and independent states...and that all political connection between them and the state of Britain is, and ought to be, totally dissolved."

Some delegates, however, were still reluctant to sever all ties with the mother country, particularly those from Pennsylvania and New York. The New England representatives supported Lee's call for independence, but they were determined not to move too quickly or too far ahead of the other colonies.

A committee was formed to draft a statement outlining the reasons for independence that might win the approval of all. Its members were John Adams, Benjamin Franklin, Robert Livingston of New York, Roger Sherman of Connecticut, and Thomas Jefferson of Virginia. The task of actually writing the document fell to Jefferson.

On July 2, 1776, the Continental Congress voted to approve Lee's resolution. The decision was a political compromise, with twelve colonies voting in favor and New York abstaining. Then the Congress took up debate on Jefferson's first draft. On July 3, John Adams wrote to his wife Abigail that independence had finally arrived, and that in the future July 2 would be celebrated as "the most memorable epoch in the history of America," if not mankind. On July 4, Jefferson's Declaration of Independence was officially adopted by the Congress.

In New York, Washington ordered a copy of the Declaration read aloud at a public meeting. In celebration, soldiers and civilians toppled the statue of George III erected to commemorate the Stamp Act repeal and melted it down, using the metal to make thousands of musket balls.

Washington's men needed all the encouragement they could get. Just days before, 127 British ships carrying Howe's soldiers from Halifax had begun arriving in New York Harbor. The British landed unopposed on Staten

Island and set up camp. It was here that they learned the American congress had voted for independence.

Howe was upset by the news. Believing the Americans had some legitimate gripes, he had hoped the colonists' differences with the Crown could be worked out peacefully. His instructions, in fact, had been to make a final appeal for peace, but his overtures to the Americans were rebuffed. For the British, peace still meant pardons for all those rebels who would renew their allegiance to the Crown. But this offer remained unacceptable to the colonists. As a result, Howe had no choice but to proceed with an attack.

Unsure of where that attack might come, Washington divided his troops between Brooklyn and Manhattan, and he waited. But Howe was in no hurry, because more troops were on the way. On July 12, a second, somewhat larger fleet arrived from Britain—commanded by the general's brother, Richard—its transports loaded with soldiers. Next, Clinton, Parker, and Cornwallis returned from Charleston. Then, finally, a fourth fleet arrived carrying twenty-six hundred British soldiers and eight thousand Hessian mercenaries.

Howe now had at his command twenty-two thousand of the best-trained, best-equipped soldiers in the world. Washington had ten thousand men. This would be no roadside skirmish.

This map of the Battle of Long Island was published by William Faden in London less than two months after the fighting. Faden shows the British troops landing at Gravesend, their march to Flatbush, and Howe's encirclement of the American left flank. With Howe were Percy, Clinton, and Cornwallis. On their minds, respectively, were Lexington, Bunker Hill, and Charleston. The rout of the outnumbered Americans was so complete that afterwards Lord Percy remarked, "This business is pretty near over."

Believing the earthworks on Brooklyn Heights to be the key to the Americans' defensive position, Howe focused his army on the southern and eastern approaches. He landed fifteen thousand men at Gravesend Bay on August 22 and slowly approached the American lines. Over the next few days, the British attempted a number of probing attacks. But the main assault didn't come until late in the evening on August 26. Howe's plan was to feign a massive frontal strike against the Americans' most forward line, while a much stronger force under Clinton, its movements obscured by darkness, outflanked this position and attacked from the rear. The plan worked. More than a thousand of Washington's troops were killed and as many captured.

The American general knew that the British would now mass for an attack on the earthworks at Brooklyn Heights, and he also knew that the Brooklyn position would most likely fall. On August 28, he ferried across the East River to inspect the lines for himself. Personally directing the strengthening of the defenses, Washington gave the impression, for the benefit of morale and the watchful British, that he had chosen to make his stand on the Heights. But secretly, he had already decided to evacuate Brooklyn at the earliest opportunity.

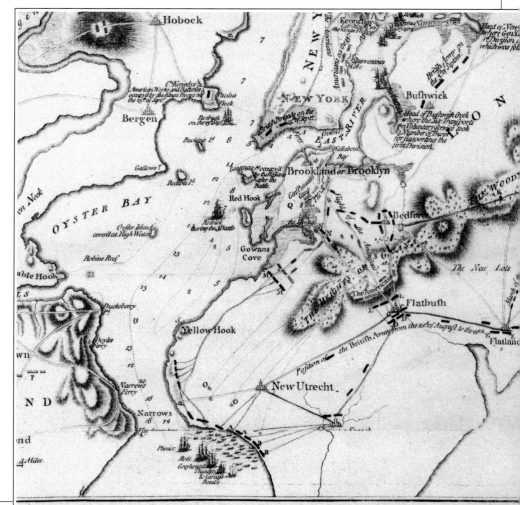

with part of LONG ISLAND, STATEN ISLAND & EAST NEW JER
the Woody Heights of Long Island between FLATBUSH and BROOKLYN on the

That afternoon, a series of violent thunderstorms prevented further British advances. All through the night and the next day, the rain kept falling. Content with their position, the British set about constructing platforms from which to begin a preliminary artillery bombardment of the American lines, while Washington continued to give every indication that his troops would defend the Heights to the last man. That evening, however, the general ordered their evacuation, instructing his officers to "impress every kind of craft...that could be kept afloat." Leaving but a handful of men on the front lines to deceive the British, the Americans hastily slipped away. As dawn approached, a welcome fog provided enough cover to cloak the escape of these few remaining companies. Washington himself was on the last boat to pull away from the shore. By the time the fog had burned off, the Americans were gone.

For a moment, Washington's army had been tightly in Howe's grip. Yet inexplicably, he had released it. "General Howe," Israel Putnam declared, "is either our friend or no general. He had our whole army in his power...and yet he suffered us to escape without the least interruption.... Had he instantly followed up his victory, the consequence to the cause of liberty must have been dreadful."

Whether it was his sympathy for the Americans, or his somewhat passive nature as a military commander, Howe rarely pressed his advantage. A number of times during his tenure as commander-in-chief, Howe possessed the means and the opportunity to obliterate Washington's army. Yet not once did he seize the day.

Despite Washington's successful stratagem, the British swiftly conquered New York City and its environs. For the same reason that he had seen fit to retreat from Brooklyn, Washington continued to avoid, whenever possible, a conclusive confrontation with Howe's potent force. While the British paraded through New York to the exultant cheers of the local Loyalists, Washington's Continentals fell back to northern Manhattan, out of the range of Howe's guns.

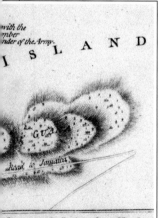

This woooden canteen belonged to Noah Allen of the Sixth Massachusetts Regiment, who was sent to Fort Ticonderoga in September of 1776.

On the night of September 20, 1776, Washington and his men watched from their encampments as the sky above New York lit up like a torch. The British-held city was on fire, and when the blaze was finally brought under control, fully one-quarter of Manhattan lay in ruins. Howe was furious, suspecting that unscrupulous patriots had set the fire intentionally.

Coincidentally, while the city still smoldered, a young Connecticut schoolmaster named Nathan Hale was brought before the general. Accused of espionage, Hale had been found carrying maps showing British troop positions.

The fire having put the general in a wrathful mood, Howe sentenced Hale to death by hanging. The next morning, Hale mounted the gallows with a now legendary composure. As the hangman made some final preparations, Hale delivered a speech in support of the cause of liberty. "I only regret I have but one life to lose for my country," he is reported to have said.

While Howe chased Washington about the southern tip of New York, a complementary threat was developing in the north. Determined to build on his victory at Quebec, the military governor of Canada, Sir Guy Carleton, had built a frontier shipyard at the northern end of Lake Champlain and constructed a small fleet there. His goal was the recapture of Lake Champlain. With control of the lake and the Hudson River, the British could effectively sever New England from the rest of the colonies.

Under Philip Schuyler, commanding general of the Northern Department, Fort Ticonderoga remained the strategic focus for the Americans in the Lake Champlain area. And Schuyler saw to it that the fort was garrisoned accordingly. In October of 1776, Horatio Gates commanded thirteen thousand men there.

Ticonderoga had originally been built in 1755 by the French to repel attacks from the south. And so that it could be easily resupplied from the friendly north, the fort was built on a peninsula that provided easy access on its northern side. The British, however, would be attacking from the north, so Schuyler took steps to remedy this weakness, ordering lines of earthworks dug along the anticipated route of the British approach.

With the war's end, Fort Ticonderoga was abandoned. There was no need for a garrison, and the country was being rapidly settled anyway. Ticonderoga's walls did provide a convenient quarry, however, and the new homesteaders carried away whatever they could, leaving the fort in ruins.

Schuyler also ordered the fortification of Mount Independence on the eastern shore of Lake Champlain, across from the fort. The Independence position would provide a crucial link to American supply depots in the Hampshire Grants. And taken together, Ticonderoga and Independence would form an impassable barrier between Champlain and the Hudson.

Despite this focus on fortifications, the Americans understood that control of the lake might be decisive. To meet the threat of the British invasion fleet, General Gates assigned Benedict Arnold to supervise the hurried construction of an American fleet at Skenesborough (now Whitehall). Between the middle of June and late August, Arnold's men produced six flat-bottomed gundalows, each of which carried three guns, and as many galleys.

Reconstruction of the fort was begun in 1906. Now completed, Fort Ticonderoga is a full-size model of its former self.

The galleys were somewhat larger ships with eight to ten guns apiece and crews of up to eighty men.

Arnold spent the month of September drilling his inexperienced sailors near the northern end of the lake. Then, on October 11, lookouts sighted Carleton's fleet. The British sailed completely past Valcour Island before they realized the Americans were lurking behind it. This ambush gave Arnold a tactical advantage, but the firepower of the British was too much for his makeshift squadron to handle. Heavy British guns pounded the Americans, inflicting extreme damage, yet they hung on tenaciously for two days. At one point, mounting casualties obliged Arnold himself to point many of his flagship's guns. In the end, Arnold's fleet was destroyed, but he nevertheless succeeded in stunning the British and, in the end, halting their advance. Carleton continued south toward Ticonderoga, but upon surveying its defenses, and considering the lateness of the season, the British commander decided not to challenge the thirteen-thousand-man garrison. Concluding that he had been delayed too long by Arnold, Carleton turned his fleet around and sailed back to the north end of the lake.

Meanwhile, in New York, Howe continued to take his time. Not until mid-October did he move to encircle the American position on Harlem Heights. And then when he did, it was with such deliberateness that the Continentals had more than enough time to escape. On October 16, Washington ordered a retreat from Manhattan across the Harlem River to King's Bridge, and from there along the Bronx River to the village of White Plains. The only troops left on Manhattan Island were those garrisoned at Fort Washington, a set of formidable earthworks overlooking both the Hudson and Fort Lee on the Jersey side.

Nathanael Greene (left) was generally a sound soldier. But for some reason, he insisted to Washington, the general, that Washington, the fort, could be defended.

Slowed by skirmishing parties that Washington had deployed along his route, the British column didn't reach the American advance position until the morning of October 28. There, American troops under General Joseph Spencer fought bravely and well, but they were no match for the British, who eventually broke the American lines. Marching in two columns, Howe's men quickly came up to the main American position. Yet rather than press the attack, Howe proceeded to dig in. For three days Howe dawdled, while Washington made plans for a withdrawal that was accomplished on the night of October 31.

According to the American general Gold Silliman, "Howe had our whole army in his power, and had he not been blinded by the directions of Providence, every soul of us must have been prisoners." Had Washington's army been captured, it is unlikely that another could have been raised. The rebellion would have ended there.

Unsure of Howe's next move, Washington reluctantly divided his force. One portion he delegated to Charles Lee for the protection of New England. Another he left at Peekskill to guard the Hudson Highlands, which controlled access to the upper Hudson and Lake George. With the remainder, about two thousand men, he crossed the river and marched south to Fort Lee.

From there, on November 16, the commander-in-chief watched Fort Washington fall. The British won a flawless victory, capturing the entire defensive force of between two and three thousand men with hardly an effort. And then, encouraged by this success, Howe promptly ordered Cornwallis to cross the Hudson and take Fort Lee. Leading a demoralized band of "half-starved, half-clothed, half-armed, discontented, ungovernable, undisciplined wretches," as a contemporary described them, Washington could not afford to risk a fight. Instead, he quit Fort Lee. And when Cornwallis attacked at dawn on November 20, the fort's commander, Nathanael Greene, pulled out, too, joining Washington at Hackensack.

With four thousand British in pursuit, the Continental Army fled south. First to New Brunswick, then to Trenton, and finally across the Delaware River to the temporary safety of Pennsylvania. New Jersey, however, was now completely in British hands.

In this painting by Dominic Serres, British men-of-war sail up the Hudson river to attack Fort Washington (on the right), defying a largely ineffective crossfire of cannonades. Fort Lee (on the left) would fall four days later. Right: "George Washington at Princeton," by Charles Wilson Peale.

THE TIMES THAT TRY MEN'S SOULS

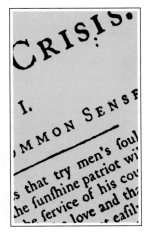

DECEMBER, 1776. To the American soldiers huddled in makeshift huts on banks of the Delaware, the future must have seemed as cheerless as the winter clouds that massed overhead. Howe's rapid advance through New Jersey had sent morale plummeting. With the British now so close to Philadelphia, even the Continental Congress had thought it wise to retire temporarily to Baltimore.

On December 19, Thomas Paine published *The Crisis*. He had written the new pamphlet at night, by the light of the campfire, while serving as a volunteer under Nathanael Greene. When *The Crisis* was finished, Washington ordered it read aloud to his troops. "These are the times that try men's souls," Paine began. "The summer soldier and the sunshine patriot will, in this crisis, shrink from the service of their country; but he that stands now deserves the love and thanks of man and woman."

Although Howe once again appeared to have victory within his grasp, the general chose not to cross the wintry Delaware. Instead, he left on December 13 for his own comfortable quarters in New York City, where he would await the spring. Along the route of his return march, Howe deployed his army of occupation. The linchpin of this chain was the advance Hessian force at Trenton under the command of a blustery colonel named Johann Räll.

Washington desperately needed a victory. His troops were safe for the time being, but they were depressed. And with the enlistment period for many soldiers ending December 31, the general feared that by spring he would be left without an army.

The week after Howe's withdrawal, a patriot spy named John Honeywell reported to Washington that Howe had indeed departed, leaving Räll in command of three Hessian regiments at Trenton. Räll, however, having little respect for the Americans, had not bothered to fortify his position. In response to a lieutenant's suggestion that they build barricades, the colonel had shouted, "Let them come! We want no trenches! We'll at them with the bayonet!"

When American reinforcements under John Sullivan arrived, Washington decided to risk an attack. He chose the night of December 25, expecting the Hessians' consumption of holiday ale to be considerable. On Christmas Day, Washington mustered his men.

They were a disheartening sight, shivering in the sleet that began to fall as the day darkened. Many were dressed in tattered summer clothing; a few had wrapped their unshod feet in rags. Here and there were spots of red in the snow—blood from their raw and punctured soles. Yet on the eve of this attack, their spirits were remarkably high. Alexander Hamilton, then but a young infantry officer, described the Continentals as "ready, every devil of them...to storm hell's battlements that night."

Harassed by the worsening storm, the crossing of the Delaware was slow and dangerous. Boats weighed down with men, horses, and artillery had to fight hard against the strong current and the ice. It took nine hours and many trips for the Americans and all their supplies to reach the Jersey shore. After that, even the prospect of facing the Hessians must have seemed a relief.

As Washington had hoped, Räll was completely unprepared for the American attack. In fact, the colonel was sleeping

---

Left: A reenactment at Valley Forge. Top right: The Battle of Princeton, as painted by William Mercer. Bottom right: An American powder horn from the Neumann Collection at Valley Forge. As the war went on, the powder horn was often replaced by the cartridge box.

when the two columns of Continental soldiers reached Trenton at dawn. There was some brief fighting as the Hessians tried to organize themselves, but the resistance was scattered. A thousand of Räll's men were captured, and the colonel himself mortally wounded, while Washington's own losses were slight.

The victory at Trenton reanimated the Americans, but it also aroused the British. Stationed in nearby Princeton, Cornwallis ordered his troops to turn out for an attack on the Continental Army in Trenton. But while Cornwallis marched south, Washington cleverly slipped past him. Instead of taking on the British in Trenton, Washington captured the supplies Cornwallis had left behind in Princeton. And keeping on the move, the Americans marched as far north as Morristown before settling in for the winter.

During this pause in the hostilities, General Burgoyne took a leave in London, where he reputedly wagered fifty guineas that England would win the war by Christmas, 1777. The key, he believed, was control of Lake Champlain and the Hudson River. Burgoyne's plan to secure these strategic waterways was soon adopted by the British authorities.

It called for a three-force campaign. Burgoyne himself would lead an army of eight to ten thousand British and German regulars down the lake to Fort Ticonderoga. From the Mohawk River country to the west, Colonel Barry St. Leger would attack Fort Stanwix in present-day Rome, New York, and continue on to rendezvous with Burgoyne at Albany. The third force would include elements of Howe's army moving up the Hudson River from New York City. But Howe's role was much less clearly defined. Further-

more, as commander-in-chief of the British forces in America, he had a great deal of personal discretion in the deployment of his men.

In fact, Howe thought he had a much better plan. Believing St. Leger and Burgoyne's forces to be strong enough without him, the British commander set his mind on the rebel congress at Philadelphia. Unfortunately for Burgoyne, Howe neglected to make these new plans clear to his subordinate, who was left waiting for troops that would never arrive.

Expecting another attack, the Americans at Ticonderoga and Mount Independence prepared as best they could. The fortifications, especially the "Great Bridge" drawn across the lake that winter, were impressive engineering achievements. But the small army stationed there was not up to the task of manning such widespread defenses. Gates had commanded thirteen thousand men at Ticonderoga in the fall of 1776, but in the early summer of 1777, Major General Arthur St. Clair had at his disposal a combined garrison of fewer than three thousand able-bodied men.

Assuming that Burgoyne would first strike at Ticonderoga with its exposed northern approach, St. Clair made plans to hold the fort as long as possible before retreating across the floating bridge to Mount Independence. These plans were scuttled, however, when the British took advantage of a serious American blunder. None of the American generals—not Gates, not Anthony Wayne, and not St. Clair—had seen fit to occupy commanding Mount Defiance to the west. They had deemed it impossible to fortify. But as one of Burgoyne's generals declared, "Where a goat can go, a man can go; and where a man can go, he can drag a gun."

His left hand sheltered Napoleon-style from the biting cold, George Washington leads his men across the Delaware River north of Trenton in this painting, an idealized interpretation by Emanuel Leutze that now hangs in the Metropolitan Museum of Art.

With General John Burgoyne presiding, the British invasion force of nearly eight thousand men moved south by brigades, averaging seventeen to twenty miles each day.

On July 5, after a perfunctory skirmish on Ticonderoga's flank, the British began to install an artillery position atop Defiance that would threaten all of the American lines. Realizing his mistake, St. Clair ordered an immediate evacuation of both Ticonderoga and Mount Independence. Moving out that night under the cover of darkness, the Americans fled south with Burgoyne quickly giving chase.

The loss, without a fight, of such carefully fortified positions was a severe military blow. But even more significant was the emotional cost to the men of surrendering the fort that had symbolized both the strength and resiliency of the nation in the north.

In a condition of stunned dismay, St. Clair's troops hastily loaded boats with provisions, ammunition, and cannon. These supplies were taken southward up the lake to Skenesborough and from there hauled overland to Fort Ann and then Fort Edward on the Hudson. Other units escaped Mount Independence by taking the supply road east into present-day Vermont. On July 7, at Hubbardton, elements of the retreating garrison fought and lost a bloody battle to a pursuing British force under General Simon Fraser. The Continentals who survived the engagement retreated all the way back to the Hudson.

For the Americans, who were used to traveling in small parties through the woods, the trip to Fort Edward was routine. But for the British, moving in force through unfamiliar swamps and toting unnecessarily heavy packs, the trek was debilitating. Hounded by American scouting parties along the way, Burgoyne and his men spent almost a month cutting a wilderness road that was not more than twenty-five miles long.

ON FIRING A MUSKET

Musket balls (1) were made from lead melted in a crucible (2) and then poured into a mold (3). Once the ball had cooled (4), it was removed, and the excess lead, or "sprue," was clipped away (5).

The powder necessary for a single shot could be measured (6) and charged by hand (7). But in battle, there wasn't much time. During the war, soldiers made extensive use of paper cartridges containing a ball and a premeasured charge of powder.

With the firelock at half cock, a small amount of powder was poured into the pan as a primer. The remaining powder was emptied down the muzzle, followed by the ball and the cartridge paper itself, which held the ball in place. The rammer forced the entire package down the muzzle.

Rifles were fired somewhat differently. Musket barrels were smooth and larger in diameter than the balls they fired, which made them easy to load. For greater accuracy, however, rifle barrels were grooved to spin each ball, so it had to fit tightly.

A piece of cloth called "patch" (8) was used to make the fit snug. It was rammed down with the ball (9), then trimmed (10).

Local militias having cleared the area of livestock and grain stores, Burgoyne's column was forced to consider other means of resupply. During the second week of August, the situation became desperate, and so did Burgoyne. He was losing so many discontented, hungry men at this point that he gave the Indians with him permission to scalp deserters. Even so, Burgoyne considered his situation to be salvageable.

Still without respect for the capabilities of the Continental Army and the spirit of the local militias, the British general detailed a raiding party. Its mission was to seize a storehouse of American supplies at nearby Bennington.

To their dismay and ultimate distress, this mixed force of German Brunswickers, British rangers, Loyalists, and Indians met a well-led and feisty force of two thousand men

under John Stark. The patriots clobbered their opponents, killing 207 men and taking about 700 prisoner. Furthermore, news of the thrashing delivered at Bennington rallied a number of patriots, who flocked to Saratoga to join the Continental Army there.

Simultaneously, St. Leger was having his own troubles in the valley of the Mohawk. Arriving at Fort Stanwix on August 2, St. Leger and his main force of approximately 1,500 men had besieged the fort and its complement of 750 soldiers under Colonel Peter Gansevoort. St. Leger then issued a demand for the fort's surrender, which Gansevoort refused. The American commander had supplies enough to last six weeks. And just in case, he had sent a request to General Philip Schuyler for reinforcements.

When news of the British siege reached him, a brigadier general in the local militia named Nicholas Herkimer mustered a force of eight hundred men to relieve Stanwix. On their march, however, they were ambushed by four hundred of St. Leger's Indian allies. The fighting was brutal, often hand-to-hand, with heavy casualties on both sides. Herkimer was forced to retreat, but the Indians also began to lose interest in

following St. Leger. When rumors circulated that Benedict Arnold was approaching with a vast army, the Indians decided it was time to go home. St. Leger had little choice but to follow. That Arnold's "huge" army numbered only nine hundred men mattered not at all in the end.

Though he could no longer expect support from St. Leger, Burgoyne nevertheless decided to press on toward Albany, anticipating the arrival of Howe's force moving up the Hudson. But Howe's thirteen-thousand-man army had instead shipped off to Maryland, whence it marched on Philadelphia.

Aware of Howe's intentions, Washington chose the banks of the Brandywine Creek for his defense of the American capital. Taking up a position near the main Philadelphia road, the general divided his eleven thousand men among the Brandywine's few passable fords. There, he waited. On September 11, 1777, Howe attacked.

The British battle plan mirrored the one used so effectively on Long Island. Five thousand men under General Wilhelm von Knyphausen executed a feint against the American center, while Howe and Cornwallis led a much stronger force on a quick march around the American right flank. The results were also much the same: Knyphausen's attack held the American front line, giving Howe's men the opportunity to take a commanding position on the American right.

But once again, Howe hesitated, giving General John Sullivan the time he needed to pivot his men and face the new threat. Sullivan's agility in turn gave Washington time enough to arrange yet another orderly retreat of the army. The evacuation of Philadelphia was much less orderly, however, as the Continental Congress abandoned the city on September 19. A week later, Cornwallis rode into town.

The Congress soon reconvened in York, Pennsylvania, where it continued to discuss the nature of a future federal government. But the loss of the capital shook the public's trust, particularly its trust in Washington. Faced with much the same situation he had confronted on the banks of the Delaware, the Virginia gentleman again opted for an ambitious attack. His target would be nothing less than the main British encampment at Germantown.

As the Hessians had at Trenton, the British forces considered the possibility of an attack so remote that they never bothered to entrench. To take advantage of this carelessness, Washington devised a complicated plan that called for the simultaneous assault of three converging columns. Moving independently at night, each column was supposed to arrive at its attack position at 2:00 A.M. on October 4. If the plan worked, the Americans would catch their foes in a vise. If it failed, the elements of both surprise and coordination would be lost.

A heavy ground fog at dawn didn't help matters any, but the Americans were already confused by then. With the exception of a division under the obviously intoxicated Adam Stephen, the Continentals followed orders. But the militia units never got into the fight at all. Anthony Wayne's division fought brilliantly, chasing companies of light infantry back through the main British camp. Wayne's

The general pictured above was known as "Mad Anthony" Wayne. The "Mad" meant daring and adventurous, however, not loony. Wayne once said he would storm the gates of hell if Washington made the plans.

men fought so well, in fact, that when Stephen's division arrived late to the field, it faced not the British left flank, but Wayne's rear. Seeing only a line of soldiers, Stephen's men fired at them. The shooting understandably caused Wayne's men to halt their initially successful advance. They couldn't understand how the enemy had gotten *behind* them.

In the meantime, the British regrouped and launched a strong counterattack, forcing the stalled Americans to retreat. Casualties on the American side were 673 killed and wounded with 400 captured. The British lost 521 men. After the battle, General Stephen was court-martialed, and his division placed under the command of a young French expatriate, a particular favorite of Washington, the Marquis de Lafayette.

O n the northern front, the Americans were doing much better. Just as Horatio Gates replaced Schuyler in command of the northern army, news of the murder of Jane McCrea on July 27 spread through the countryside. McCrea was the fiancée of a Loyalist officer serving under Burgoyne. As the story goes, a number of Indian scouts began arguing over who would have the honor of escorting the lady into the British camp. In the heat of the dispute, one of the scouts shot and scalped her. Even though she had been a British sympathizer, New York patriots were nevertheless outraged, and they blamed Burgoyne.

With this new determination among his men, and the return of Arnold from Fort Stanwix, Gates now commanded an army of some seven thousand men. Taking into account his losses at Bennington, Burgoyne could count on fewer than six thousand men. And then the British commander received the worst news of all. He learned that Howe had sailed for the Delaware Bay on July 23. No relief would be forthcoming from New York.

The battles of September 19 and October 7 were fought along the western shore of the Hudson River, four miles north of Stillwater, New York. The Americans were encamped by a town then called Saratoga, but now known as Schuylerville.

At 10:00 A.M. on September 19, the British began a tentative advance on the American position atop Bemis Heights, south of Saratoga. Because the area was so hilly and thickly wooded, Burgoyne could not get a clear picture of the American deployments.

Knowing that the British right flank was vulnerable, Arnold begged Gates to let him attack. At length, Gates agreed and sent a troop of riflemen under Daniel Morgan and a company of musketmen under Major Henry Dearborn against the British advance. Morgan's men met the British at Freeman's Farm. Using the Freeman buildings and some of the woods for protection, the Americans fired

at the redcoats, who were grouped together in the clearing. Then, as the British charged, Arnold brought the rest of his division forward, and a general engagement followed.

Arnold sent a messenger to Gates informing the general that, with a few reinforcements, he could overrun the British. But Gates cautiously delayed committing more men to Arnold's fight. Even so, Arnold's unrelenting attacks threatened to lick the British altogether until the Baron von Riedesel arrived with five hundred reinforcements to drive

The Breymann Redoubt, shown in this diorama, was a single line of breastworks about two hundred yards long and some seven feet high. Named for Lieutenant Colonel Heinrich Breymann whose German troops were stationed there, this temporary fortification guarded the British right flank. Benedict Arnold's leg was injured during one of the assaults on the redoubt, which was captured by the Americans during the fighting on October 7.

the pugnacious Americans back. When Gates finally did send reinforcements, they were too little too late. As the day ended, the British controlled the field. But the "victory" was an empty one. They had lost six hundred men, and there was still Gates's army to contend with.

On October 5, Burgoyne called a council of war and proposed an all-out attack on the Americans. When his generals pointed out that such an attack would be risky because the terrain prevented proper reconnaissance, Burgoyne suggested a reconnaissance-in-force to probe the American left. If it proved weak, the reconnaissance could be expanded into a more general attack.

In the meantime, on the American side, Gates and Arnold were feuding. Jealous of the glory that Arnold had won for himself at Freeman's Farm, Gates petulantly refused to mention Arnold's name in his official dispatches to Congress. When a raging Arnold confronted him on the matter, Gates used this insubordination as an excuse to relieve Arnold of his command. Arnold then threatened to write Washington requesting a transfer, but Gates called his bluff. Knowing that the dance with Burgoyne would soon resume, Arnold instead retired to his quarters and waited for the British to advance.

Marching out of Freeman's Farm on the morning of October 7, the fifteen hundred British and Germans under Simon Fraser could see very little. But the Americans, on higher ground, could see the British quite clearly. Benjamin Lincoln, the division commander who replaced Arnold, attacked with great suc-

cess. Arnold himself was confined to his quarters by order of Gates, but when he heard the grunt of battle in the distance, he seized a horse and galloped onto the field, which had quite likely been his plan all along. Though without any official authority, Arnold assumed command by general consent of those present and relentlessly assaulted the enemy. Gates, back at his headquarters, sent a messenger with orders insisting that Arnold leave the field.

Under Arnold's leadership, the Americans surged into the British center, mortally wounding Fraser and chasing his men back to their fortifications at Freeman's Farm. Pursuing them hotly, Arnold fought hard to take the enemy's redoubts. First, the Breymann Redoubt fell. Then, later in the evening, the Balcarres Redoubt was evacuated by order of Burgoyne.

During one of these assaults late in the day, Arnold was unsaddled by a musket ball that hit him in the left leg and killed the horse beneath him. The leg was the same one Arnold had injured during his attack on Quebec New Year's Day, 1776.

It was as Arnold lay bleeding on the field that Gates's messenger finally reached him. But the order directing Arnold to return to his quarters arrived too late. The battle had already been won. At first, Burgoyne, abandoning his sick and wounded, tried to run. But seeing that flight was useless, the British commander surrendered on October 17.

At Valley Forge, more than a thousand huts were built within a matter of days. The men, Tom Paine wrote, were "like a family of beavers, every one busy." Measuring fourteen by sixteen feet, the shelters held twelve bunks each. Straw, moss, and mud were used to chink the log walls.

furmount every difficulty w
tience becoming their pr
caufe in which they are e
fhare the hardfhips, and pa
nience.——

After his defeat at Germantown, and with the British occupying Philadelphia, Washington needed to find a suitable location for a winter camp. It had to be close enough to keep an eye on the British, yet far enough away to discourage a surprise attack—and on land that was easily defensible. In the end, Washington chose Valley Forge, a day's ride from Philadelphia, on high ground, and protected by the Schuylkill River and Mounts Joy and Misery. The Continental Army arrived on December 19, 1777, and immediately set about constructing huts and fortifications. With its population of twelve thousand, the Valley Forge encampment became, instantly, the second largest city in North America.

The soldiers suffered from the usual shortages of supplies, lacking adequate food and clothing for much of the winter. But though the winter was punishing, it was not remarkably cold.

On February 23, 1778, the Prussian Baron Friedrich von Steuben arrived in camp. A specialist in military drill, von Steuben took on the formidable task of transforming the Continental troops into a uniform, well-ordered army. He began in late March by standardizing the close-order drills that tended to vary from command to command, depending on the part of the country the men were from. Although he knew no English and worked through interpreters, von Steuben nevertheless managed to complete America's first military manual. And by spring, his work paid off in a well-drilled force that would fight more efficiently on the march as well as in battle.

Baron Friedrich von Steuben (left), who spoke both German and French, would sometimes call to one of his aides in the language of Lafayette: "Come and swear for me in English. These fellows won't do what I bid them."

'f in   re,
ntry.   ent
leneral to take post in
np, and influenced by
at the officers and sol-
mind, will resolve to
a fortitude and pa-
ion, and the sacred
ed. He himself will
e of every inconve-

"Unless some great capital change takes place," Washington wrote of the supply problems at Valley Forge, "...this Army must inevitably... Starve, dissolve, or disperse, in order to obtain subsistence in the best manner they can."

VICTORY

AMONG HIS MANY distinctions, Benjamin Franklin was a frequent guest of the French court at Versailles. The French and Franklin liked each other, in part because they both despised the British. As early as 1775, Franklin beseeched King Louis to intercede in the Revolutionary War on behalf of the Americans. But the French monarch demurred. His government would encourage the colonists and even provide them with considerable quantities of covert aid, including arms and money. But to have France enter the war openly was simply too much for Franklin to ask.

French policy, however, did not bar individual citizens from joining the Americans, and many rallied to the patriot cause. One of those drawn by the patriots' romantic, republican ideals was the nineteen-year-old Marquis de Lafayette. Upon hearing news of the Battle of Bunker Hill, the young nobleman wrote, "The moment I heard of America, I loved her; the moment I heard she was fighting for freedom, I burned with a desire of bleeding for her."

Washington took a particular, and somewhat paternal, interest in Lafayette, who returned the commander's affection. At first, Lafayette offered to serve without pay, wishing only to be "near to the person of General Washington until such time as he may think it proper to entrust me with a division of the army." That time came at Valley Forge, Congress having previously bestowed upon Lafayette the rank of major general.

Meanwhile, in Lafayette's homeland, news of the magnificent American victory at Saratoga reached the French court on December 4, 1777. Quickly, the French attitude changed. If the Americans could so completely overcome Burgoyne, it was reasoned, then perhaps the time had come to recognize American independence officially. On February 6, 1778, the two sovereign states signed a Treaty of Commerce and Alliance. By June, England and France were at war.

As the French made preparations to enter the war, General Howe left it, resigning of his accord in favor of Henry Clinton, who became the supreme British commander in May of 1778. Under orders from London, Clinton organized an immediate withdrawal from Philadelphia that began on June 18. The British authorities wanted to focus on the French in the Caribbean, so Clinton would have to run things from the main British base in New York.

From his headquarters at Valley Forge, Washington considered what to do. Spring had brought with it fresh provisions and the will to take the offensive. Assessing the situation, Washington decided his men were fit enough to challenge the British.

Dispatching a small force under Benedict Arnold to enter Philadelphia, Washington led the main body of his troops north in pursuit of Clinton. For a week, the Americans paralleled Clinton's course through New Jersey. Then, on June 27, Washington ordered Charles Lee ahead with an advance force to attack the

The "Marquis de Lafayette" was the man's title. His given name was Marie Joseph Paul Yves Roch Gilbert du Motier.

British rear. Lee personally believed that the Americans should play it safe, allowing the French to take over much of the fighting. But Washington's orders were direct and unambiguous.

The next morning, Lee marched up on the British rear a few miles north of Monmouth Court House. Once the

Benjamin Franklin (above) was probably the most sophisticated man in America, as urbane as any Parisian. Yet for the French, he played the simple farmer, an agricultural version of Rousseau's "natural man." Franklin even went so far as to wear a beaver hat on occasion.

This painting by Emanuel Leutze shows Washington (with the sword) relieving Lee (on the white horse) at Monmouth Court House. According to General Charles Scott of Virgina, who was there, Washington swore at Lee "till the leaves shook on the trees."

Charleston and its environs. Originally called Charlestown, this South Carolina seaport was the scene of two momentous British expeditions, the failed invasion of 1776 and the successful siege of 1780 (shown at right).

A 1778 British rebus (shown below) imaginatively entreats Americans to forswear a French alliance and cease their rebellious ways.

skirmishing began, Washington's second-in-command took to issuing a stream of scrambled, ill-advised orders. Units were moved from one position to another for no clear purpose. Soon Lee's field officers became understandably confused, and slowly, they began to fall back. The British, sensing the Americans' disarray, pursued.

When Washington rode ahead of the main force to check on Lee's progress, he was startled to find elements of Lee's command in all-out flight. When he found Lee, Washington demanded an explanation. None was forthcoming, save Lee's argument that an attack at this time was not prudent. In a rare loss of composure, Washington roared at Lee that he expected his orders to be followed. The court martial would come later. First, Washington set about rallying his troops in order to avoid a rout.

Galloping among the lines and shouting words of encouragement to the soldiers, Washington managed to reform them into a defensive posture that held long enough for the main army to come up. Von Steuben's recent training notwithstanding, Monmouth proved once again that the Continental Army could fight well if well led. Monmouth was also the last major battle to be fought in the northern colonies. The balance of the war would be decided in the south.

Despite the specter of the French, and the earlier setback at Charleston, the British remained convinced that the south was thick with Tories whose support, if harnessed, could change the course of the war. Charleston remained the greatest prize, but its natural and manmade defenses were substantial.

On December 29, 1778, the British gained a footing in the south, capturing Savannah, Georgia. Then, in June of 1779, Major General Augustine Prevost led a column from Savannah against Charleston, calling upon the city to surrender. When Governor John Rutledge refused, Prevost made plans for a siege. But the arrival of a Continental force under Benjamin Lincoln forced the British to retreat.

Calling upon the French fleet for aid, Lincoln pursued Prevost to Savannah. Thirty-five hundred Frenchmen under

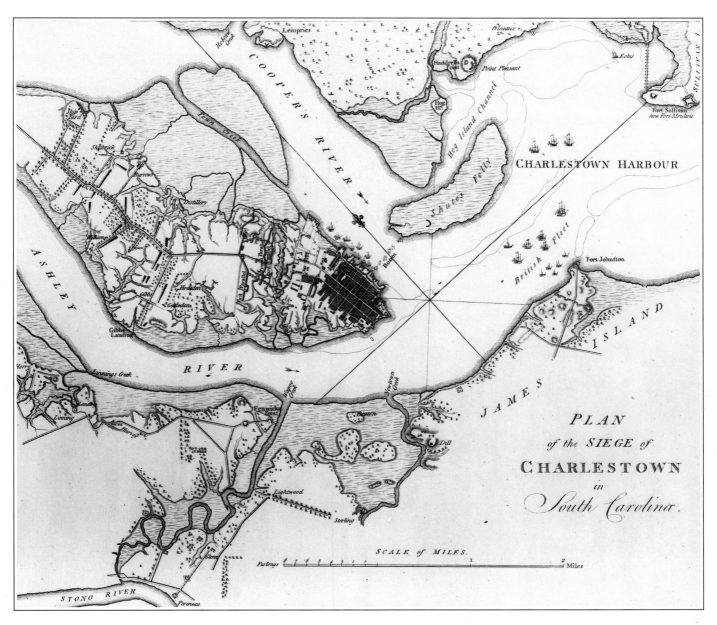

PLAN
of the SIEGE of
CHARLESTOWN
in
South Carolina.

SCALE of MILES.

Admiral Charles d'Estaing arrived at Savannah on September 12, joined by Lincoln and fifteen hundred Americans four days later. Together, they began constructing siege lines. By October 9, however, d'Estaing had grown worried that his fleet might be vulnerable to a British attack while it lay moored within Savannah's inland waters. Motivated by this fear, he insisted on storming the city's fortifications immediately. When the ill-conceived plan failed, the French raised the siege. And with little else to do, Lincoln marched his men back to Charleston.

The next move was left to Clinton, who sailed from New York City on December 26, 1779, with eighty-five hundred soldiers aboard ninety transports. His destination was Charleston.

After riding out some ghastly weather off Cape Hatteras, Clinton's force landed thirty miles south of Charleston on

February 11, 1780. The Americans had fifty-four hundred men on land and some seven warships in the harbor, but these ships were so inferior to the British fleet that four of them were sunk intentionally to block the mouth of the Cooper River.

On March 29, Clinton crossed the Ashley River and began regular siege operations. Meanwhile, fourteen British warships moved into Charleston Harbor past a renamed Fort Moultrie that surrendered without a fight.

Because Charleston was located on a peninsula, Lincoln had arranged an escape route for his men across the barricaded Cooper. But a British division under the ruthless Banastre Tarleton drove Isaac Huger's cavalry from the Cooper's north bank, thereby cutting off any breakout and trapping the American army in Charleston. On May 12, after weeks of thunderous British bombardment, Lincoln

TREASON

The most famous American traitor in history, Benedict Arnold moved toward his fate as inevitably as any Shakespearean character. Following his appointment as military governor of Philadelphia in May, 1778, Arnold began courting the city's social elite, including the Tories. A year later, the thirty-eight-year-old widower married Peggy Shippen, a Tory half his age whose taste for lavish entertainment far exceeded Arnold's means. With her aid and encouragement, the American general, obsessed with his country's ingratitude, began a secret correspondence with the British authorities, offering to switch sides in exchange for a large sum of money.

In the summer of 1780, Washington offered Arnold an important field command in the upcoming campaign. But Arnold turned him down, citing the leg injury he had received at Saratoga. Instead, Arnold asked for command of the garrison at West Point. Because it guarded the crucial Hudson Highlands, the fort at West Point was strategically crucial to the Americans and highly coveted by the British, with whom Arnold's correspondence continued. The courier assigned to Arnold was a young British major named John André.

On the night of September 21, 1780, emissaries from Arnold rowed out to meet the British sloop *Vulture* anchored twelve miles below the fort. André was taken aboard and carried back to the western shore, where Arnold was waiting. Together, they discussed plans for Arnold's betrayal of the fort.

But dawn broke before André could return to the *Vulture*, forcing the major to return with Arnold to the house of Tory sympathizer Joshua Smith. It was assumed that André would return to the ship once darkness could again cloak his movements. But later that morning, the *Vulture* was discovered and fired upon by an American shoreline battery. His river escape cut off, André would now have to return to New York by land. Smith exchanged André's British uniform for a civilian suit, while Arnold issued him a pass in the name of John Anderson.

Top: Major John André is hanged in a scene from George Bernard Shaw's play, The Devil's Disciple. *Above: Benedict Arnold cleverly persuades André to hide the secret plans in his boot.*

arrytown, however, André was seized by a
ting party. Believing the men were
André foolishly revealed himself. When he
mistake and produced Arnold's pass, it
too late. He was taken prisoner, and dur-
rch that followed, plans of West Point's
ere found hidden in his boots.

a few days before some confused American
re able to recognize Arnold's treachery,
ch time the traitor fled to safety aboard the
ndré, however, was imprisoned as a spy and
to death. Anxious to save his friend, aide,
é, Clinton protested this extreme punish-
offered to free any prisoner of war if
were spared. But the only deal
n would accept was Arnold for André, an
hat Clinton could not make if the British
to encourage future desertions.

iful man by nature, Washington was
s convinced that justice demanded André
ate of Nathan Hale, who had been captured
lar circumstances. On October 2, 1780,
vas hanged. "I pray you to bear me wit-
id, snatching the noose from a hesitant
r and placing it around his own neck, "that
fate like a brave man." Arnold, for his part,
mething over £6,000 and a general's com-
the British army.

PLAN
des Forts, Batteries
et Poste de West-Point.
1780.

*This chain formed part of a boom
that blocked the Hudson at West
Point (see map above).*

capitulated, surrendering his entire army to Clinton. The
new southern strategy appeared to be working.

For the Americans, Charleston was a hugely demoraliz-
ing defeat. They lost thousands of men, tons of supplies,
and their most defensible base in the region. And with
Charleston secured, Clinton was able to return to New
York with the preponderance of his army, leaving
Cornwallis in charge to pursue the southern campaign.

To oppose Cornwallis, the Continental Congress selected Horatio Gates, who was quickly dispatched to rebuild
the Continental Army in the south. In the public's mind,
Gates was, above Arnold, the hero of Saratoga. Gathering
together four thousand men, mostly militia units, he decided to march immediately against a British outpost at
Camden, South Carolina. There, Lieutenant Colonel
Francis Rawdon commanded a combined garrison of one
thousand British regulars and Loyalist militia.

When news reached Charleston of Gates's advance,
Cornwallis personally led a column of one thousand reinforcements to Camden. And then pausing only to muster
Rawdon's men, the British commander moved out to inter-
cept Gates. The two armies skirmished briefly during the
night of August 15, 1780, but withdrew until morning.

With the rising of the sun, Cornwallis's outnumbered
army attacked the American left. Putting up almost no
fight at all, the militia units there fled, often leaving behind
their loaded, unfired muskets. Next, the British turned on
the Continentals, eventually scattering these unsupported
troops, who fought bravely until overwhelmed. Gates personally disgraced himself by running from the field, and
once again the American army in the south was destroyed.

Having thus secured South Carolina, Cornwallis
began preparations for a full-scale invasion of
North Carolina. But while the army established its camp in
Charlotte, a legion of one thousand Loyalists under Major
Patrick Ferguson was dispatched to put down rebel activity
in the Appalachian Mountains. To oppose the British, the
mountain men raised their own force of a thousand men
and marched down on Ferguson's camp at Gilbert Town.

At first, Ferguson retreated back toward Charlotte. But
at Kings Mountain, just across the border in South
Carolina, he turned to fight. Ferguson had taken up a
strong defensive position on the thickly wooded hill. But
on October 7, the Americans, after surrounding Kings
Mountain, crept up its slopes Indian-style and began pick-
ing off Loyalists from the cover of the woods. Ferguson led
his men in a number of successful bayonet charges, but
each time the Americans rallied. In the end, the Loyalist
column was annihilated, convincing Cornwallis to abandon
his plans for North Carolina.

On October 6, 1780, Major Patrick Ferguson wrote to Cornwallis, "I arrived today at Kings Mountain and have taken a post where I do not think I can be forced." Ferguson was wrong.

After Cowpens, chronic rheumatism forced Daniel Morgan to resign his commmand and return home to Virginia.

After Kings Mountain, Cornwallis fell back to Winnsboro, South Carolina. Meanwhile, after his shameful performance at Camden, Gates was replaced by thirty-nine-year-old Nathanael Greene.

During December, 1780, Cornwallis and Greene shadowed each other, each general dividing his forces. The American commander sent Daniel Morgan to the west with a third of his army, while Greene himself went south. Cornwallis sent Tarleton after Morgan, then moved north to cut off Morgan from Greene.

Tarleton caught up with Morgan on January 17 at the Cowpens. Acknowledging the lesson of Camden, Morgan decided not to group the militia units by themselves on one flank. Instead, he chose to organize his troops into three parallel lines of defense: a skirmish line of sharpshooters, a second line of militia, and a third line of Continentals. Morgan never

Halberds were carried by sergeants mainly to signify their rank, but spontoons (second from left) were still used in combat, as were linstocks (third from right), which held the matches used in firing cannons.

expected the militiamen to hold the British regulars. In fact, their orders were to fire three good volleys and then withdraw. Not trusting to the chain of command, Morgan spent the night before the battle personally touring the camp and explaining the plan to his men.

Once the action began, Morgan's sharpshooters quickly reduced Tarleton's officer corps. Then the militia units fired their three volleys and began to retreat. Thinking that a rout was developing, the British surged forward, only to be routed themselves by a Continental cavalry charge. It took just over an hour for Morgan's plan to work to perfection, and by the end of the battle, the Americans had captured or wounded more than eight hundred of Tarleton's eleven hundred men.

But Morgan was not out of the woods yet. Cornwallis still lay between his army and Greene's. And the British commander, furious with the news of Cowpens, was out for revenge. Moving quickly, Cornwallis thought, he could squash the Americans and, at the same time, free Morgan's 525 British prisoners.

With Cornwallis at his heels, Morgan fled north on an angled march for a rendezvous with Greene, whom he joined at Guilford Courthouse, North Carolina, on February 8, 1781. Rather than fight Cornwallis, Greene decided to continue the retreat to Virginia. But when Cornwallis gave up the chase, Greene moved cautiously back across the border. And when reinforced, he took up position again on some high ground back at Guilford Courthouse.

Borrowing Morgan's tactic, Greene set up three parallel lines of troops, with the less dependable militia units up front and the sturdier Continentals again in the rear. Cornwallis attacked on the afternoon of March 15, about one o'clock.

Having marched twelve miles to reach the battlefield, the British were already tired. Fighting through three lines of Americans only added to their fatigue.

At first, it seemed as though the Guilford result, too, might be a reprise of Cowpens. But at the third line, the British broke the Second Maryland Regiment and turned the American left flank. At this point, the momentum had clearly shifted to the British, but the Americans counterattacked with such success that Cornwallis was forced to fire his artillery into the fray. The anti-personnel grapeshot killed as many redcoats as it did Continentals, but it did stop the American advance.

At this point, with the issue unresolved, Greene chose to withdraw. As at Bunker Hill and Freeman's Farm, the British were left holding the field, but at an appalling cost. The 500 British killed, wounded, or missing, compared to 79 Americans killed, were more than one-quarter of Cornwallis's entire command. Parliamentary opposition leader Charles James Fox suggested that "another such victory would ruin the British army."

"I HAVE NOT YET BEGUN TO FIGHT !"

COMPOSED MOSTLY of privateers who indulged in a form of legalized piracy, the Continental Navy was a fairly inconsequential force, most effective in raiding British merchant shipping and never willing or able to take on British ships of the line. When France entered the war in 1778, however, King Louis was kind enough to provide his allies with a few refurbished warships, among them the *Bonhomme Richard*, named after the "Poor Richard" of Franklin's famous almanac. Its captain was a Scottish outlaw named John Paul who, having escaped to America, added the alias of Jones.

In the most dramatic naval encounter of the war (and perhaps in history), Jones with his forty-gun ship engaged the fifty-four-gun British *Serapis*. The battle took place off the southeast coast of England during the summer of 1779. It should have been no contest. The *Serapis* was state-of-the-art, the pride of the British fleet, alongside which the *Bonhomme Richard* seemed an aging, patchwork embarrassment. Yet through luck, fortitude, and a great deal of guile, Jones was able to take the measure of her.

The battle strung out over many hours as the two ships jockeyed for advantageous position. At one point, when the destruction of the *Bonhomme Richard* seemed imminent, an aide to the British captain called out to Jones, inquiring about a surrender. So close were the ships that the indomitable captain was able to shout his response. According to legend Jones yelled, "I have not yet begun to fight!"

Knowing that their only chance was to board and seize the *Serapis*, the desperate Americans hung on until finally an explosion on the British gun deck forced Captain Richard Pearson to strike his colors. The victory, if the result could be called one, belonged to Jones, although the issue might be better termed one of survival. During the course of the four-hour battle, half of Jones's three-hundred-man crew was killed or wounded. And the hull of the *Bonhomme Richard* was so badly shot away that, at certain points, a cannonball could pass all the way through the ship without hitting anything.

"Long before the close of the action," Captain Richard Pearson wrote of his engagement with John Paul Jones (center), "it became clearly apparent that the American ship was dominated by a command will of the most unalterable resolution."

Above: Earthworks outside Yorktown. Right: Washington at the Yorktown surrender, from the painting by John Trumbull. On his march south to Williamsburg, Washington made a short detour to Mount Vernon. Until then, he had not slept in his own bed for six years—not since he left for the Second Continental Congress in 1775.

Following Guilford Courthouse, Greene moved south to continue his mission of harassing British troops in the Carolinas. Ably assisting him were guerrilla forces under the "Carolina Gamecock," Thomas Sumter, and Francis Marion, the "Swamp Fox." Although marked by battlefield losses, Greene's own campaign kept the British occupied, allowing Washington to isolate Cornwallis.

Convinced that Lord Rawdon could handle General Greene by himself, Cornwallis marched eastward from Guilford Courthouse to the port of Wilmington on the North Carolina coast. There, he was resupplied by sea, and after resting briefly, he pointed his army north toward Virginia.

Cornwallis had now become convinced that taking Virginia was the key to ending the rebellion, because such a victory would effectively cut off the southern colonies from the north. He was particularly confident because the Chesapeake Bay and Virginia's many navigable rivers provided excellent landings for a water-borne army, and the Royal Navy still dominated the coastal waters.

In advance of Cornwallis, Clinton sent a raiding party under Benedict Arnold, now a British brigadier general, to the Virginia seaboard. Arriving at Hampton Roads on December 20, 1780, Arnold's men proceeded to loot the countryside and burn much of Richmond. Eager to capture Arnold and prevent further pillaging, Washington dispatched Lafayette with twelve hundred men. They arrived in mid-March.

Playing high-stakes poker, Clinton added to the build-up by tossing another twenty-six hundred troops into the Virginia pot. Cornwallis himself arrived in late May, bringing the number of British scattered about Virginia to

upwards of seven thousand men. With five thousand men himself, counting local militia units, Lafayette indulged in some skirmishing with Cornwallis's unified command. By late summer, however, the skirmishing tailed off, and the British settled into the deep-water port of Yorktown, while Lafayette occupied nearby Williamsburg. The next moves would be naval.

During the summer of 1781, George Washington coveted New York. Having kept the British bottled up there for two years, while putting down occasional mutinies among his own poorly fed and unpaid soldiers, the American commander was anxious to act. He was tired of helplessly watching Clinton from the Hudson Highlands. But Washington needed help to take New York—specifically, the help of four thousand French troops under Rochambeau and the French fleet under de Grasse.

On May 21, Washington met Rochambeau in Wethersfield, Connecticut, where the two of them agreed on a plan for assaulting Clinton in New York. Privately, however, Rochambeau believed Cornwallis's position in Virginia to be the proper focus of a joint attack, and he secretly wrote to de Grasse suggesting that the French fleet sail to the Chesapeake Bay. On August 14, Washington received a message that de Grasse was indeed headed for the Chesapeake. The American general was furious—"tossing like a suppressed volcano within," according to one of his lieutenants. But he had little choice if he wanted his de Grasse's aid.

On August 21, Washington and Rochambeau began moving their armies carefully to the south. It was important that Sir Henry Clinton receive no early indication of their intentions. To that effect, Washington went so far as to build bread-baking ovens for a French encampment that would never exist. This deception and others fooled Clinton, who didn't catch on to the troop movements until September 2. By then, there was little he could

do to help Cornwallis. On August 30, the French fleet had dropped anchor in Chesapeake Bay.

Control of the sea was crucial to the joint French-American operation. With it, Cornwallis would be trapped in Yorktown. Without it, the British could either aid the general in an attack on the besieging armies or evacuate his men if that became necessary. What the generals did on land would matter little. It was the naval battle off the coast that would decide Cornwallis's fate. The French fleet boasted twenty-eight warships; the British fleet, when it arrived on September 5, numbered nineteen ships of the line. That afternoon, the two navies engaged. Two hours later, they separated, and several days later the French returned to their anchorage outside Yorktown, while the British fleet returned to New York. Cornwallis was trapped.

Washington and Rochambeau's men arrived at Williamsburg in late September, joining Lafayette there. On September 28, the combined French and American force of 17,600 men removed itself to Yorktown. During the next two weeks, Cornwallis was slowly squeezed by the encroaching American lines.

Using well-coordinated raids to inch their siege artillery ever closer, Washington and Rochambeau made the British position progressively less tenable. Yorktown was bombarded both day and night from within four hundred yards of the British lines until, finally, the disheartened British general could no longer stand the shelling. On October 15, Cornwallis wrote to Clinton that his situation was critical.

On the morning of October 17, a British drummer boy scaled some earthworks and beat out the signal for a parley. As the American and French guns halted their barrage, the boy was joined by a British lieutenant waving a white handkerchief over his head. The last British military force actively campaigning in North America was about to capitulate.

Cornwallis declined to attend the formal surrender. Pleading ill health, he sent General Charles O'Hara, who

attempted to submit to Rochambeau. But the Frenchman simply shook his head and gestured to Washington. "We are subordinate to the Americans," he said.

For all practical purposes, the war ended at Yorktown, but a formal peace was still two years away, because King George refused to accept Yorktown as anything more than another setback. Within five months, however, the ministry of Lord North was toppled, and his successor, Lord Rockingham, immediately opened negotiations with the Americans. On November 30, 1782, preliminary articles were signed, terminating all hostilities between the British and the Americans. Then another year passed while Parliament and the Continental Congress debated these articles, delaying formal ratification of the Treaty of Paris until September 3, 1783.

While Franklin, John Adams, and John Jay negotiated for the Americans in Paris, Washington marched his victorious army north, where it could once again keep watch on Clinton in New York. Meanwhile, Greene besieged Charleston, and Anthony Wayne surrounded Savannah. Once peace negotiations began, however, holding these towns meant little to the British. Savannah was evacuated in July, 1782, and Charleston in December. But New York City itself wasn't surrendered until the peace treaty was formalized.

After years of wishing it were so, George Washington finally entered New York at the end of November, 1783. On December 4, he met with his general officers at Fraunces Tavern in lower Manhattan. The occasion was a farewell party. Washington was resigning.

"Men who have risked their lives in a common cause are bound together by the strongest of ties," historian Page Smith has written. "They share the incommunicable memories that will die only with them and that, in not a few instances, merge with the common memory of their nation, passed on from generation to generation.... With all their faults and shortcomings, this small band of heroes had, in the end, prevailed and persevered."

George Washington epitomized these men who had risked all for the ideal of liberty. His fortitude, his insight, and most of all his patience had kept the fledgling nation, time and again, from losing its way. It is sometimes difficult, through a cynical modern prism, to imagine the heroic potential of a single man, but Washington himself should not be underestimated. Whatever may be said about Saratoga's importance as a turning point in America's war for independence, the day that George Washington arrived in Cambridge to take command of the Continental Army was the day that Fortune smiled on the nation.

Ω

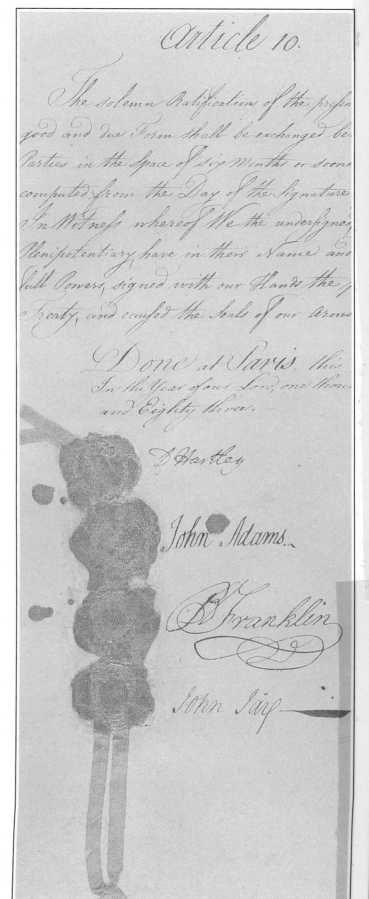